# The paradox of freedom in everyday leadership practice

An inquiry into the identity work of developing leadership in the public sector in Denmark.

**Rikke Horup Sørensen**
**April 2021**

Submitted to the University of Hertfordshire in partial fulfilment of the requirements for the degree of doctorate in management

Rikke Horup Sørensen

# The paradox of freedom in everyday leadership practice

Forlag:  BoD · Books on Demand, Strandvejen 100,

2900 Hellerup, bod@bod.dk

Tryk: Libri Plureos GmbH, Friedensallee 273,

22763 Hamborg, Tyskland

ISBN: 978-87-7691-369-4

# Abstract

This thesis is an autoethnographic inquiry into the identity work of leaders working in the public sector in Denmark. The research is about how degrees of freedom can be experienced when it is acknowledged that leaders are paradoxically both enabled and constrained through interdependencies with others. The main puzzle is about what is involved in the processes of leaders negotiating identity when thinking about the mutual constitution of individuality and sociality.

This research argues that identity work within leadership is based on contradictions and ambiguities as well as how leaders simultaneously form and are formed by social rules and norms. The inquiry illustrates the temporality of leadership identity. It emphasizes how the human capacity to adapt to different power relations comes with either the risk of indeterminacy and a weak sense of self or with the risk of determinacy and a weak sense of the other. Losing the paradoxical understanding of these interdependencies might result in either dogmatism or relativism. This research provides critical insight into both positions. Relying on a mixture of collaborative autoethnography and reflexive narrative inquiry, I research into my own practice of leading and facilitating leadership development. The research is problem-driven and based on an exploration of experiences of my interactions with the people I work with.

The paradoxical approach to identity leads to a perspective on freedom, which acknowledges the ongoing interdependencies between individuals and their relationships with others. The understanding of freedom in this thesis is opposed to the idea of freedom as liberation from the constraining character of our relationships with others. I argue against an understanding of freedom *from* constraints and emphasize how freedom can be found within interdependent and constraining relationships. This research considers how I and other leaders, both formal and informal, can find degrees of freedom *to* engage with how we are continuingly both enabled and constrained and improvise within these entanglements. The inquiry emphasizes the importance of resonant relationships with others in the processes of negotiating identity based on the assumption that humans more fully recognize themselves in relationships with others. Resonant relationships and the perspective on the mutual interdependencies within the leadership identities that emerge might enable us to find ways to move on in everyday leadership practice.

In this research, I suggest that the ongoing exploration of the emergent power relations, in which we get caught up, and the rhythms of work as navigation through time and space are important in understanding the emergent identities – regarding both the self and others. Through such inquiry, we might be able to negotiate and find greater room to manoeuvre, in this thesis emphasized as a position of *being with oneself in another*.

Further, the research presents an argument of how contemporary idealisations about leadership and organizational life might create problems regarding our sense of freedom when leading. An important aspect of leadership is to explore the character of our interdependencies.  Such an inquiry takes time, where the perceived need for speed within the organizational life can be a stumbling block.

Further, the idealisation of individual freedom, that comes with the demand for self-management, builds on an understanding of autonomous individuals, and a perspective on humans as resources, which breaks with the paradoxical approach of this thesis. Paradoxically the experience of some degree of freedom comes, in the arguments presented within this thesis, by acknowledging the ongoing enabling and constraining character of the emergence of leadership identities.

**Key authors**: N. Elias, M. Foucault, C. Mowles, R.D. Stacey, A. Honneth, G.H. Mead, M. Merleau-Ponty, R. Bernstein, H. Lefebvre, H. Rosa

**Keywords**: Leadership, identity work, paradox, freedom, indeterminacy, rhythm analysis, resonance, power, idealisation

# Acknowledgments

I owe my thanks to the University College of Copenhagen for financing this research, to Pernille Thorup for introducing me to the Doctor of Management Programme, and to my manager Ghita Vejlebo for supporting my endeavours.

My sincere thanks to the Doctor of Management research community, both students and faculty, for continuingly rich and challenging conversations.

 A special thanks to my two supervisors Emma Crewe and Chris Mowles, for their dedication and priceless inspiration, encouragement, and constructive critique, and my learning set colleagues, Helle T. Stoltz, Sune B. Larsen, Nama Sidi, and Beate Midttun, for your collaboration through curious, challenging, and supportive conversations.

Thank you to the clients and colleagues I work with, both those who gave their consent to show up in my narratives and those with whom I have shared and tested out my findings along this research process.

Finally, I express my gratitude to my family, especially my two sons, Lukas and Vitus, for their unconditional love and always supporting me in following my dreams – even when it means spending time away from the family.

# Table of content

# Introduction

This thesis consists of a collaborative and reflexive encounter with myself and others about my working practice and the people with whom I have been working over the last three years and six months of conducting research at the Doctor of Management Programme (DMan). When I joined the DMan, I came from a tradition of working within a social constructionist approach to my work within leadership development.  This approach was based on a belief in humans forming the future together through dialogue. Even though this was, at the time, an important foundation of my practice, I had begun to find how this perspective left me stuck at times and without a sense of agency in my work. I was eager to find out whether I could find alternative ways to think about my own involvement within the field of leadership and how this might enable me and others to find new ways of moving on in our work.

With hindsight, I see now how the strong emphasis on the enabling elements came from the appreciative paradigm, with the assumption that we can positively form the future, which is closely connected to social constructionist ideas. What I experienced as "stuckness" was closely related to the absence of reflecting on the constraining elements of everyday organizational life.

When I started to inquire into these blind spots in my own sense-making, this became emotionally disturbing for me in my research process. I felt anxious when I experienced having my professional identity challenged.

Looking back, this experience was the stepping stone to progress with my research. It helped to clarify the research theme of exploring how leaders struggle for freedom and agency and how these processes are closely connected to identity.

Several scholars have in recent years argued that understanding what public leadership in Denmark concerns has become progressively complex, based on arguments about how ambiguities have become an increasingly part of the defined tasks for public leaders. (Pedersen, Greve & Højlund, 2008, Åkerstrøm Andersen & Grønbæk Pors, 2014, Kaspersen & Nørgaard, 2015). There is an emphasis on how these demands form an increasingly unclear ground for public leadership. Some scholars even refer to the consequences of the contradictory character of the expectations of leaders as a leadership crisis, pointing towards the results that leaders struggle to live up to various roles and demands at the same time. (Kaspersen & Nørgaard, 2015). The emphasis is on how leaders must self-manage to find ways within the unclear and elusive character of their task. At the same time, leadership is also about how to develop the capacity of self-management in others (Åkerstrøm Andersen & Pors, 2014:16).

My research takes an approach that explores how leadership emerges in these conditions and how to understand the processes for the leaders involved. Becoming reflexively aware has enabled me to better understand the contradictory expectations of leadership.

## Occupational context

Since 2011, I have been an employee at the department for leadership at the University College of Copenhagen – the first three years as an assistant professor and subsequently as an associate professor. The cornerstone of our work is to offer post-graduate education to leaders, primarily working in the public sector. The students come from different leadership positions in their everyday organisational work-life and different educational backgrounds, e.g., nurses, teachers, social workers, etc., and join the programme to supplement their professional background with a leadership perspective. In the first years of my employment, my primary tasks were developing different courses and teaching.

Over the years, adjacent assignments have been an increasingly large part of my everyday life. The generic perspective on leadership has been substituted with a high demand for tailored leadership development in specific organizational contexts with concrete challenges. Such assignments carry elements of teaching leadership, focusing on facilitating dialogues about specific organizational needs for changes, which leads me to take more of a consultancy role.

In recent years, I have experienced requests for continuing conversations with leaders, both individually and in groups, who feel the need to share their struggles within their everyday leadership practice to find ways of moving on in situations when they feel stuck.

As an employee at the University College, I have experienced an ongoing focus on efficiency and thinking in terms of turnover in comparison with competing educational institutions and consultancies. We now talk just as much about clients as about students. This movement has impacted our focus on the internal development and marketing of our products. Shortly before I joined the DMan, the University College of Copenhagen went through a merger, which led to experiences of uncertainty for the other employees and me in our sense of what we might become in this new organization. My many years of teaching, consulting, and close relationships with public managers often bring me into processes of ongoing adjustments of our education and develop new concepts or leadership programmes for specific challenges. Such development activities have also included more research-like tasks, such as literature reviews and authoring chapters of books about leadership. As a result of the merger, the redefinition of how to work in the department of leadership also became an increasingly significant task for me.

In this sense, my work entails taking on multiple roles and thinking about my practice. I think of myself as a multi-roled practitioner. My everyday interaction is mostly related to leaders, both the students, clients, conversation partners, and the leaders at the University College, which has led me to think about my own practice – also in terms of taking a leadership role. I experience similar demands for self-management in my work, as the above-mentioned scholars suggest (Pedersen, Greve & Højlund, 2008, Åkerstrøm Andersen & Grønbæk Pors, 2014, Kaspersen & Nørgaard, 2015). When teaching, facilitating, or as a conversation partner, I find myself taking a role as a temporary leader.

I have enjoyed the opportunities to take on different roles and assignments, and I have felt highly recognized for my ability to take on various tasks in our department. I get bored easily, and I have found it important to be able to take on new challenges and innovations in my way of working.

Traditionally, the approach to the work within leadership at the University College has been highly influenced by social constructionist ideas. Working from the perspective of forming the future by talking positively about it with inspiration from appreciative inquiry, which I will explain further in my project one, has helped leaders formulate their visions for the organisations within which they work. However, I have found it difficult to engage with the more conflictual elements of organisational life. I have often experienced frustration when the future did not develop as I (or the managers I work with) wished for. I have come to question the social constructionist focus on the future and the strong emphasis on language. What about the body? How might beings be formed by history and not only becoming who we are in future relations? To find ways of practicing leadership in the above-mentioned ambiguities in which public leaders are to self-manage, is one of the issues I have been puzzled by in my work.

## Research theme

My collaborative capacity to take on multiple roles and adapt to changing demands has been a significant part of my professional identity. The freedom to self-manage my way of doing this process has felt important to me. A simultaneous struggle to belong to many groups, and a need to stand out as an individual, has come up several times in my autoethnographic and reflexive account of the ongoing themes in my work life. In this research process, I discovered how my entanglement in a search for both a sense of belonging and freedom was an ongoing theme and how this theme is not only about me but seems to be reflected in the identity work of the leaders I work with and the community of researchers I have collaborated with in the Doctor of Management Programme (DMan).

The ongoing reflections on this struggle have evolved into the following theme for this research:

***An inquiry into the paradoxical and contradictory experience of freedom and constraint within the social process of negotiating leadership identity.***

My research is about how the simultaneous struggle for freedom and belonging in social communities is played out as processes of identity work in the practice of leadership. I explore how the relationship between individuals and social communities to which we belong can be understood and how our interdependency with others can be intertwined with a sense of freedom as an individual.  My inquiry is closely connected to my understanding of the conditions in Denmark, and in our more specific sectors and localities, within which public leaders and I must navigate everyday organizational practice.


## Research approach and thesis structure

This thesis seeks to inquire into this research theme from a multidisciplinary perspective, more generally inspired by an approach to understanding everyday organizational life as complex responsive processes of human relating (Stacey, 2003, 2009, 2012, Stacey & Mowles, 2016). The DMan is a professional doctorate is based on this perspective, which has emerged from various disciplines such as group analytical thinking, complexity sciences, process sociology, and pragmatic philosophy, as explained by Mowles (2017). The students are encouraged to inquire into their own practice by taking their own experiences as research objects. The idea is to explore puzzling aspects of our everyday professional experiences and to present these through narratives in four projects and combine the arguments in a final synopsis. The narratives within the projects present a reflexive account of my practice and serve as the empirical foundation of the analysis and present experiences of breakdowns in my practice. The idea of my research is to frame situations of breakdowns as a mystery, which, according to Alvesson and Kärremann, can be seen as the first step towards resolving a breakdown (2011). The narratives are chosen from experiences in my practice where I feel unable to make sense of the situation or stuck in my moving on with others. It is presented as a puzzle to explore and the research can, in this sense, be seen as problem-driven, which is why I do not start with a formal literature review. Instead, a wider range of literature is reviewed as the research progresses, inspired by the themes arising from the narratives.

The main theories I draw on are brought in because they are helpful for inquiring into my practice and based on James´ understanding that true ideas are those ideas we can verify through the concrete difference they make in one´s actual life (1907:92). My dissatisfaction with the social constructionist approach in finding ways to practice leadership has led me to explore theories that emphasize aspects on which social constructionists seem to miss out. Among others, I inquire into aspects of thinking paradoxically about individuals and the social environment based on Hegel, Elias, Mead, and Mowles, which also allows an additional perspective on power and challenge, a strong focus on language with Merleau-Ponty and Lefebvre´s perspective on body, time, and space.

The approach of the DMan requires writing four projects, where project 1 is an intellectual autobiography, giving an account of me as a researcher, the main influences of my life and how I became who I am, and how this background is influencing my everyday practice at work. The subsequent three projects consist of reflexive narratives from my practice followed by an analysis of the puzzling aspects of my experiences. With inspiration from autoethnography (Ellis, 2011), the projects combine autobiography and ethnography with narrative inquiry. Each project stands for itself and is left unchanged after finishing it. In this way, the projects reflect the progression of my thinking about the research as it moves on. The purpose of keeping the chapters unrevised once completed is so that the readers and I can appreciate the iterative development of thought and practice. The reflexive process of writing the projects is reinforced in the final synopsis, where the methodology of the thesis is presented in more detail, and the progressive arguments of the projects are taken into a further reflexive turn. The concluding arguments and contributions are finally presented in the end of the thesis.

The DMan is based on a highly collaborative community in which students are obliged to participate. We all attend four residential weekends a year. We are divided into smaller learning groups of four people and a supervisor, with whom we attend four meetings a year. The learning sets continuingly read and comment on each other's works and share conversations about the research - both at the residentials and in ongoing virtual meetings. The methodological approach in my thesis is further elaborated in the synopsis, which illustrates the iteratively emerging process of the choice of methods used in this thesis.

After this introduction, a presentation of the four projects, followed by a synopsis, constitute the structure of this thesis.

# Project 1 – The contradiction of belonging and freedom

## Introduction

Project one is a reflexive autobiography, in which I intend to reflect on how I have come to think the way I do today, from my experiences in my (working) life and the development of my professional identity through my interaction with the world around me.

My autobiography is being reflected and articulated with the perceptions I have today and thereby selected in a way that makes sense in this temporal perspective. The choices of some and not other experiences will only be part of my story and they will be based on contingent choice and represent a reduction of the complexity in the experiences by which my way of thinking has developed. Through this writing process, I also hope to discover new patterns and storylines. With this hope, I connect to this quote by Michel Foucault: ”*I don´t feel that it is necessary to know exactly what I am. The main interest in life and work is to become someone else that you were not in the beginning. If you knew when you began a book what you would say at the end, do you think you would have the courage to write it? What is true for writing and for a love relationship is true also for life. The game is worthwhile insofar as we don´t know what will be the end*” (1982a:1).

Even though I write about my past, the communication about it creates new perspectives on my experiences. It creates openings for reflection on alternative interpretations and maybe even new possible identities. This approach illustrates an ongoing learning process that I hope to illustrate and continue in this project.

## Family background

In 1972 I was the firstborn child of my parents. Three years later, I had a baby sister, and the four of us lived as a family in a small city just outside Aarhus, the second-largest city in Denmark. Both of my parents came from the countryside, went to school for only seven years and were educated through apprenticeships and company training. Being a family was the top priority of my parents, and the cohesion as a family was based on a strong urge to help each other across the entire family of grandparents, aunts and uncles. My parents' jobs were also based on helping; my father was a rescuer in the local ambulance team, and my mother worked in childcare. Being helpful and putting oneself at the disposal of others was, and still is, essential in our family. We were expected to care for each other, and I was always taught to consider other people's well-being.

Another essential way of thinking in our family was based on the Danish idea of *the Law of Jante* (Sandemose, 1933). The *Law of Jante* are described in this novel and presents life in a small town in northern Jutland with a specific pattern of group behaviour. The norms entail a critique of individual success and convey the idea that individual achievement is inappropriate to show publicly. The way it was taken up in my family was based on the understanding that *you should not think you are something special – don´t ever think of yourself as better than others.*

As a child, I learned when to speak, when not to speak, and that I had to contribute when I spoke up. I remember a saying in my family about people who spoke *only to keep their mouth warm*, which referred clearly to unappreciated behaviour. I also remember talking to my father about the informal rules guiding us on how to behave. He talked about how he could not buy the expensive cars we both loved, even though he might be able to afford them. He told me that people would start talking, positioning him as a person who wanted to show off, and he implicitly told me that he would not want that to happen. I felt that I was expected to behave legitimately, not showing off and not even pretending to be better than anybody else. I found it unfair that we should accept the limitation of our freedom and the ability to do whatever we loved. My father talked to me about these things in the most loving way. He wanted to teach me these norms to enable me to avoid making mistakes and standing out. My problem was that I wanted to be included in the community, but at the same time, I also wished to stand out.


## Discovering alternative communities of practice

During my early school years, I encountered different ways of living in families and being in the world in general. I was curious about the alternative lifestyles I could observe, and in my hobbies, I was constantly trying to discover new exciting disciplines. Being into sports was a natural thing in my family, so I did not turn my back on the traditions. However, I supplemented with activities such as performing theatre, which was not typical and did not fit very well into the *Law of Jante* and the norms of not wanting to stand out. Even though it was far from what my parents knew or appreciated, they always accepted me in pursuing my dreams. I did not often quit the activities I joined, so at some point in my younger years, I participated in badminton, handball, ballroom dancing, a choir, the local theatre group, and took piano lessons – at times doing all of them at once. Therefore, my curiosity made me quite busy, and I found it easier to say yes to new activities than to leave old ones behind. Looking back, I can see this as a way of opening different possible identity constructions and beginning to form as a person who could easily adapt to different communities of practice. In this way, I found myself still living up to the rules and norms in my family and supplementing my identity by not totally accepting the typical limitations.

## Belonging – being free

I begin to see a pattern of belonging and, at the same time, not embedding all of the limitations that came along with being a legitimate member of a group. Instead, I see that I adapted some of the fundamental values. Then I moved into new communities, curiously looking for new inspiration or new values in the making of my identity. This pattern also seems to become visible through my choice of high school. I chose the old high school in Aarhus based on old traditions connected to the upper class and the artistic and literary disciplines. Choosing this high school introduced me to families with values different from mine. The parents of my friends were highly educated, worked a lot, and had many ambitions of their own. These parents had a professional identity I did not recognise from my own family. My parents worked to make money and take care of our family and create a secure environment for my sister and me.  In some of the families I met through my high school friends, the parents had a strong professional interest in their job and seemed to be motivated by personal success and professional excellence at another level than to make a living. Still, they were loving people, and most of them also had learned the lesson of the *Law of Jante*, which meant that they did not think too highly of themselves and did not show off. At the same time, there were visible differences between my family and the more career-oriented families, e.g., the cars they drove and the houses in which they lived. It was almost considered more acceptable in my family that people from academic families could choose cars and houses at a higher economic scale than my parents, who belonged to the working class.  Their ambitions inspired me, and the greater sense of freedom I felt, at that time, came along with the higher positions. I wanted to live more like this myself, but I did not distance myself from my own family values. There was a strong feeling of belonging in my family, but at the same time I wanted to belong to something else as well.

The pattern is not only about belonging. I also see a pattern in accepting and connecting to different people and different kind of values and traditions. My upbringing based on the *Law of Jante* might have been the reason why I found it difficult to be critical towards others. I felt strong belonging in my family, but I did not accept the limitations that were entailed with a "full membership". My perception that it was not acceptable to criticise others made me find ways to live up to both family norms and values and, at the same time, combine them with other ways of living. In this way, I tried to avoid criticism by adapting to the most fundamental norms in different communities. The learning from this showed that not totally belonging was not the same as being excluded, and by being somehow in between, it was possible to find a way of belonging and being exceptional.


Education
The impact of my bachelor's degree in economics at Aarhus Business School was to engender resistance as much as new knowledge. The Business School environment was characterised by students with briefcases, motivated by being successful and motivated by making money, which corresponded poorly with my ambitions of making a difference by helping other people.

Also, only a few of the courses made sense to me. There was a lot of mathematics, law, computer science, and finance – and as far as I could tell at the time – I was sure that this was not like the work I wanted to do.  We learned how to do consolidated financial statements, analysed yield curves and calculated different kinds of funding. I remember all the teachers using the phrase "*All things being equal….*" frequently. I found the approach demotivating because we all knew that these *"things"* would never be equal in real life, so I did not see the point in even doing these calculations.

I found a slight interest in only a few courses, such as organisational studies, national economics, statistics, and consumer behaviour, even though these did not take my breath away in the way that I wanted. Studying organisations and consumer behaviour touched on humanism in the approaches because these topics considered more than quantitative aspects. Still, many of the courses were very much based on the organisation's view and the nations as things or machines. We learned to analyse and understand organisations with different kinds of structures and think about organisational culture inspired by, e.g., Edgar Schein (1985). Schein suggests that organisational culture can be analysed by focusing on artefacts, values and assumptions, where only the artefacts are visible. His idea that organisational life was more complex than immediately visible and possible to capture appealed to me. Even though this perspective indicates that organisations are also about human behaviour, which resonated with my own more humanistic interests, I found that the way we were introduced to this approach was still a tool to control or fix problems. The projects we worked on defined a problem, and based on the theories, we analysed and concluded how these problems could be handled. Similar to these approaches was a perspective on organisations as machines with different elements to be analysed to make changes.

In general, the tradition of the Business School's academic approach was built on the understanding of the neutral observer. We learned to understand and analyse but did not address that we were different people doing these analytics differently. I found that I was offered a position as a professional standing outside my work field, trying to understand and analyse how to deal with a reality of which I was not part. The thinking I was introduced to, and disassociating myself from, was based on quantitative research and analysis of organisations and society. The studies aimed to make students and the people working in organisations as objective and neutral as possible.

The instrumentalised approach based on the principles of scientific management, e.g. by Taylor (1914), focused on rationalisation based on research, or Weber's theory of bureaucracy as a legitimate way to dominate in a nonpersonal law system, where people are expected to obey the laws (1968). Learning from statistics and economic models and the direct use of theoretical frameworks I encountered at the Business School to identify organisational problems and solve them corresponded poorly with my ambitions as an individual to influence some development in concrete areas. It would mean that I should strive for a position where I should see myself as a significant and influencing participant, which was very far from what I was raised to do. I was not able to articulate to myself or others at the time as to why this perspective at the business school felt so wrong. I remember not liking the professional identity I was offered. However, I found myself in no position to criticise the academic world, which made me question my ability to become scientifically competent and therefore belong to this community.

I struggled to find better alternatives but did not find any, so I decided to finish my bachelor degree. Even though I wanted the academic degree, economic studies made me realise that there were limitations to my curiosity and open-minded approach to different communities. There was something that I was not able or willing to relate to as meaningful. Reducing organisational life to numbers, accounting, margins, quantitative analysis that we (the students) could only participate in as observers or analysers was not meaningful to me. Maybe this was because it would be too disturbing to my ambitions to stand out and make a difference in the world, maybe because my family background had given me important relationships, maybe because my linguistic and social studies in high school had taught me that not all the important things in life could be measured. Some elements from my background helped me to take a critical approach to business studies by choosing not to continue my education in this direction.

Today I think about my economics studies in a somewhat different way. Even though I could not relate to the environment and the way of thinking, it was not in any way a waste of my time. Because I was stubborn and continued the studies, it provided me with a specific set of perspectives, ideas and concepts when working in organisations, which was unfolded in a certain kind of language. Being familiar with this kind of language has been useful to me ever since, as I continue to meet these perspectives in my work life and find it much easier to communicate in these contexts. I did not reflect on this at the time. However, the experience also taught me that you can join in without belonging or being exactly like "the others" as long as you know the rules and the paradigms and that resisting adapting is not that dangerous.

Moving on to study sociology and Human Resource Management

After my bachelor, I continued my education at Copenhagen Business School with a master´s degree in Human Resource Management (HRM). Joining this programme, I met two different groups of teachers. Both groups focused on humans in organisations, but the one group had what I would call a more business-oriented approach to the human factor. Here we were introduced to people as a strategic resource in organisations, focusing on the human factor to make more profit. We read classical theories of motivation, such as Maslow (1954) and Hertzberg (1959) and tried out psychological tools such as Belbin's group analysis and Myers-Briggs type indicators. All were introduced as tools to increase the organisation's efficiency. This psychological approach considered the human perspective, but it was based on an individualised view of people in organisations. People were seen as resources and the effort expected was to try to change the employees to fit in and achieve organisational goals. The other group of teachers had a critical approach to the traditional understanding of HRM. Some HRM literature dehumanised the employees by thinking of them as only a strategic resource in the organisation, which was seen as problematic. Some of our professors argued that this was an instrumentalised and reductionist way to understand humans in organisations (Steyart, 1998). This thinking resonated with my difficulties of connecting to the instrumentalised understanding of organisations, so my inspiration during these years was based on this group of teachers. Another impact on my thinking was an introduction to the interpretive paradigm (Burrell & Morgan, 1979). Here was a description of a scientific method that recognised the person developing the knowledge as a subject and underlined the importance of understanding the process of creating knowledge as an interpretation.

Communication and learning became a central theme during my master's studies. We learned that an increasing rate of change in the environment created an increasing need for learning in organisations. The importance of communication and learning activities across contexts was underlined in several of the readings. (e.g., Schein, 1993, Putnam, Phillips & Chapman, 1999). A sociological approach to organisational life underlined the contextual theme. Here we were briefly introduced to Bourdieu, Luhmann, Foucault and Habermas as possible ways of understanding the cultural elements and contradictions between contexts. It was brief introductions to what I later learned were complex perspectives. I found it difficult to combine these theories into my own understanding of organisational life. The different approaches and the different sociological perspectives did not seem clear to me at the time. However, I was drawn to these ways of investigating dynamic relations in organisations and society. All of these authors presented, in my view, valuable insights to deepen my understanding of organizational life.

Organisational learning became more and more interesting to me. I chose to supplement studies at CBS with classes in pedagogical psychology at the Psychology Institute at Copenhagen University because I wished to get out of the business school to connect with this context and combine the approaches. Here I was introduced to individual learning theory by, e.g., Piaget (1973) and Rogers (1961). Being presented to and inspired by both the individualised psychological approach to learning processes and the more sociological theories at CBS, the combination of the individual agency and the relation to the social structures became the main topic for my master's thesis to try to combine these perspectives. Writing my master's thesis, I made an effort to understand learning, therefore, from both an individual and a social perspective. I intended to understand the concept of competence development in an organisational context. I used the inspiration from Bourdieu and his ideas on economic, cultural and symbolic capital ( 1991 & 1995).

I began to understand the social as different communities with different rules, norms, values and understandings and connected this to more individual learning theory based on the understandings of Piaget (1973) and Odd Nordhaug (1993). This thinking was still based on the assumption of a dichotomy between individuals and the social but provided an understanding that interpreting what was considered competent behaviour was contextual and temporal. The impact on my thinking was that individual learning processes were affected by what was socially found acceptable and meaningful in a specific context. Therefore, the process of learning had to reflect the socially constructed understandings of what it means to be competent and not competent in the specific organisation, which should be continuingly negotiated and renegotiated depending on time and place.  To emphasise this point, I was inspired by Lave and Wenger's (1991) social theories of learning. Lave and Wenger drew my attention to how learning should be considered an integrated part of people's everyday social life in different communities of practice. They define a community of practice as

> *...a set of relations among persons, activity and world, over time and in relation with other tangential and overlapping communities of practice. A community of practice is an intrinsic condition for the existence of knowledge, not least because it provides the interpretive support necessary for making sense of its heritage.* (Lave & Wenger,1991,98).

Etienne Wenger's continued work on communities and practices and his exploration of learning, meaning and identity (Wenger, 1998) was the foundation of my further understanding and unfolding of competence development as a social process in organisations. This theory combined the two perspectives that I focused on during my master's studies into a more integrated perspective on the individual's psychological view and its "inner" processes and social processes in the organisations. I knew that there was a strong connection between the two. At this point, I understood that the main focus when working with competence development should be on the interrelation between them.

Looking back, I see that I still based my perspective on a dichotomy between the individual and the social. I conceived of the individual processes as adapting to different social contexts, and my thinking was still influenced by the instrumentalised understanding that I wanted to criticise.

At CBS, I also met a different learning environment than I was used to from the business school in Aarhus. We were a smaller group of students, and the classes were held in more intimate classrooms than the large auditoriums I knew earlier. That provided more dialogues with the teachers and the other students instead of just attending one-way communication lectures.

We were sometimes placed in large circles. There were no literature presentations but facilitation of a dialogue about how we understood the literature and how it impacted us. This kind of learning environment inspired me, and I found that in these conversations, I was invited into a group of equally legitimate participants - an alternative to the more asymmetric relation to the teachers trying to add more knowledge to the students still based on a more scholastic tradition. The experience with the dialogical and symmetric communication approach to learning impacted me because I found this made room for my own reflections and perspective, so I brought this experience with me to my later work with the facilitation of learning. In the sense of belonging, I found that these dynamic processes suited me well, and looking back, I see that meeting subject to subject was central to my feeling of belonging.


## Working as a professional

In my first full-time job after finishing my master's, I was employed as an internal consultant in a Danish trade union, organising several groups of people employed in the public welfare sector, more specifically, the professionals with either a short education or no education at all.

I was hired as an HR consultant, and my main responsibility was to find out how the organisation could design their approach to developing its employees' competencies. From the beginning, I found my task both meaningful and motivating. I tried to translate my theoretical approaches and transform them into practical initiatives to facilitate learning and organisational change. I facilitated dialogues between all organisational members to co-create an understanding of what competencies would be needed in the future. Based on these dialogues, we developed competence profiles for each job category. I intended that these profiles should be used as a foundation for the ongoing dialogue and should create a common language in the organisation to work with learning as a social process in everyday life.

I was quite satisfied by how I transformed my knowledge from the HRM studies into concrete practice tools at that time. However, it was my experience that only a few of the managers and employees actually transformed their everyday practice; my sense-making was based on my observation of how they kept on talking about competence development from an individualistic perspective and primarily focused on the educational training they wanted or used training activities as a way to reward the employees they thought were doing a good job. The competence profiles were used as a static description of expectations to the employees and helped measure whether the employees were competent or needed development. I see now that we tried to predict the future and the needs for development activities.  I contributed to this understanding by creating and facilitating communication about what would be required competencies among different job categories, and at the same time, trying to determine that a set of profiles would be a helpful tool for everybody.

In retrospect, I understand why nothing turned out the way I wished. Even though I had tried to facilitate a renegotiation about how to think of and work with competence development in the organisation, I had to accept that the new meaning had not occurred to many leaders and employees. It seemed that developing competence among the employees was still based on the same understandings as before. I see now that I positioned myself as the facilitator of these processes, trying to impact and change the organisational beliefs, by making my colleagues objects of my intentions and understandings. I did not discover that I was also part of the discourse that I was trying to challenge. I did not reflect on the culture I was participating in – I took the expert position on working with competence development. I was frustrated that my colleagues did not find it meaningful. I see now that the instrumentalised perspective on humans in organisations that I criticised during my time at CBS had become dominant in how we all worked with competence development.  The way we tried to predict the future failed and I found how no one can predict the future. At the same time, I found that the conversations about competencies and learning processes did change during these years of work. Competencies and changes in demands for employees were suddenly issues about which everybody talked. The interaction around competence development profiles did not contribute in the ways we expected, but it does not mean that it did not make a difference. I see now how the idea of competence is based on the idea that we are billiard balls, cut off from our everyday experience with each other and with a set of skills inside us.

The longer I worked in this organisation, the more I was aware of the organisation's implicit norms and discourses. From my perspective, the intense focus on solidarity and cohesion as a reason for members to join the trade union did not appear among the employees. The trade union politicians reflected a more individualised and competitive organisation – people taking care of their individual interests, resulting in power struggles and individuals or groups fighting for their perspectives. Our communication was based on discussions on the right way to think about and work with leadership and learning when meeting leaders in the organisation around the topic of competence development. Every leader defended their own perspective and was not open to others' perspectives, including mine. Because I was located in the HR department, I observed these "power games" and tried to navigate between them. However, looking back, I can see that I was also working very hard to legitimise my position and perspective. I became part of an individual fight for my own position. I found it challenging to combine my academic background with everyday life. My experience was that using academic language (that I had only just learned) was not considered appropriate. I was able to talk in another language, trying to fit in, but again I found myself in a situation where I did not want to adapt to all the unwritten rules and found that I did not contribute to the changes I would have wanted. It seemed that I was being socialised in an environment I did not like and trying to position myself in opposition. I found that I was only supporting the existing power structures. My experiences, ambitions and wish for belonging had changed over time. At first, it all seemed straightforward, and later I realised that being part of this organisation made some things possible and others impossible. I found myself stuck, and I could not find another way out other than to leave.

After my resignation from the union, I started working as a self-employed consultant. While I was self-employed, I carried out different kinds of consultancy work in different organisations. In the beginning, most of the jobs were in the private sector, but after the financial crisis in 2007 many of the private sector development processes I was involved in were closed down. Over time I got more and more jobs in the public sector. After several years, I contacted by Danmarks Forvaltningshøjskole, a public but still autonomous school that offered postgraduate education to public sector managers and employees. I went to a meeting at the school, where the responsible consultants presented their approach to leadership education. Mostly they had a strong theoretical focus on a relational perspective on leadership, which seemed to fit with my own understanding, and we agreed that I should teach part-time in this postgraduate programme for leaders in the public welfare sector. I found that most of the other jobs I had were short term tasks – often joining an organisation for one or a couple of days to facilitate some process before leaving again. Often these kinds of jobs did not leave me with the slightest idea of the impact I may be having, which I found unsatisfactory.

Teaching in the leadership programme meant working with the same group of leaders in different parts of the Danish public welfare sector for one and a half years. We focused on three themes during the programme: Personal leadership, Leadership & employees and Leadership & organisation. We worked with a specific curriculum, and most of the literature was influenced by theories I knew from my Master studies. The learning perspective from the chosen literature was based on social sciences and did not address or teach a specific way to exercise management and leadership. It provided the students with different perspectives on organisational behaviour and power mechanisms. Through these approaches, the students were to reflect on their own sense-making and choices of action.  I found a big difference between having read many of the theories or references to them and being able to translate them into specific contexts of public leadership.

The theories we worked with presented different perspectives on the conditions that public leaders were to navigate in (Pedersen, 2008, Åkerstrøm Andersen, 2001, Danelund, 2005, Danelund & Sanderhage, 2009). Most of these theories were inspired by Luhmann and Foucault's ideas, theories I knew in brief from my CBS studies. Jørgen Danelund was one of the founders of the leadership programme and he drew attention to the relationship between the practice of public leadership and the social environment in which it was carried out. With Luhmann's systems theory, Danelund tried to observe the public sector as a specific system based on specific communication methods and a sense-making based on the systems-specific codes (Danelund, 2009). Danelund's interpretation and translation of Foucault became central for my own understanding of leadership during this period. The understanding of power and discourse offered a new understanding of the individual leader as being both formed by and forming the social at the same time. This perspective resonated with my earlier experiences about belonging and my wish for freedom and became central to my way of thinking.  It inspired me to work with the students to reflect upon which discourses we were all formed by and forming in our own organisations and how they could lead and develop their leadership practice to meet the problems they faced.

The overall perspective on the leadership programme at the time was built on ideas from social constructionism. The inspiration from these ideas was developed with people from the leadership programme and from meeting people from the Taos Institute, especially Kenneth Gergen, Sheila McNamee and Harlene Anderson, and their thoughts on social constructionism resonated well with my earlier experiences. They did not present social constructionist ideas as opposed to traditional paradigms, such as functionalism, phenomenology, system theory, etc. They presented it more like kind of a meta-perspective, including the other perspectives as different truths. Harlene Anderson talks about social constructionism not as a paradigm but as a philosophical stance and I found that my whole philosophical stance for my professional approach was sharpened by these understandings (Anderson, 1997). Gergen and Gergen draw a picture of the world as a multiverse built on many truths and perspectives with no perspective more valid than another, but with power relations determining local contextual truths (Gergen & Gergen, 2004). The construction of the many truths becomes visible to us in our language, and at the same time, the language constructs truths in a dialectic process. The understanding is that we cannot observe the world from an objective position, and the subjective perspective is relationally based and becomes visible through our language. This perspective also addresses a focus on the relationship in which we articulate and construct the reality perspective. Dialogue and how to meet in the dialogical practice across contexts with other people and ourselves become central in this approach based on a temporal approach to human identity development in a becoming-perspective. This perspective indicates that people develop, and their identity emerges from different relational practices of communication (Gergen, 2009). The understanding resonated in every way with my own thinking, and the focus on relation and relational practice combined the individual and the social. In these ideas, there was no individual without the social and vice versa (Gergen, 2009). Therefore, the static way of thinking of identity is replaced by an understanding of the self, consisting of many different relationally formed selves. This way of thinking had a significant impact on me because I began to look at myself and others as incomplete and, in this way, always in the process of becoming somebody new. I did not question these ideas at the time but was drawn into this specific perspective to understand how to include these ideas in my practice.

## The influence from the students

In contrast to my earlier experiences with the *Law of Jante*, teaching invited me to take the expert position of a teacher. I worked harder than ever. I was prepared to present at every class with thousands of slides. I felt a huge responsibility for my students' learning and I was so afraid that I would not be able to explain correctly or run out of words to communicate the topics. I was also afraid of the students not getting good marks in the exams, so I put a lot of effort into this job. Again, I felt motivated and obliged to help my students, and in the beginning, it felt more like my responsibility that they learned something. This viewpoint changed over time because I experienced that I could not facilitate learning *for* the students. However, I could facilitate *with* them, which also made the learning process a joint responsibility. The students' responses to our readings were different when they had to present the theories or pick elements that they found interesting and relevant compared to when I made a presentation. I found myself more open to the dialogical interpretation based on the readings instead of transferring my understanding to the students in a didactic way. I see now that it took me some time to free myself from the understanding that the teacher was not the only expert who should present the way to understand leadership. However, just as I experienced at CBS, I found it more helpful to participate in the dialogue, present my own perspective, and be open to others´ interpretations. Being so well prepared over time also provided me with the room to act unprepared and situated. I can see a balance between feeling safe or secure enough to experiment, act intuitively, and remain open to learn myself.  After a while, it felt like a game. Playing with the theoretical texts in dialogue with my students also eliminated the dualism in my thinking theory and practice. I assumed that we constructed new meaning through dialogues based on the theories, combining them with our different experiences and perspectives. The ambition was to bring new meaning to the practice of public leadership and the theories about it. Through these dialogues, the theoretical concepts could become part of our thinking about our practice. For instance, a core topic as managing strategy did not present one way of working strategically but introduced different kinds of managerial paradigms (Danelund & Sanderhage, 2012). Through these different perspectives, we tried to observe our own organisational environment and reflect on the different alternatives to address what would make sense in our own practice. I had no experience with the practice of public leadership. However, through the dialogues with the students, I was offered a lot of knowledge about their experiences and their perspectives on their tasks.

As I got deeper into the theoretical themes about conditions for public leadership and I used the same way of thinking to challenge my way of teaching and I tried to teach the leaders to develop their leadership. In a collaborative dialogue, we reflected on the theoretical approaches the literature presented to us. I found myself both being the teacher, who presented the theories, as well as joining the reflections and the sense-making to let the new understanding affect our practice. In these conversations, we talked about leadership, and in my own reflections, I was a leader in the classroom, and the others were leaders somewhere else. These experiences have influenced my way of thinking - both about leadership and teaching as a collaborative practice, a practice performed from several positions, and learning as a relational, co-created and reflective practice. Working with leadership and learning based on this makes me reflect on these two disciplines as interactive processes. In both, we relate closely with other people, with whom we create different dynamics and negotiate how to create meaningful processes together. Bettina Rennison (2004) describes leadership as an empty concept that needs to be given meaning repeatedly and based on a powerful historical construction. In leadership and learning processes, I found that we constantly have to explore what is needed in a specific situation. With inspiration from John Shotter's theme about 'withness' (2015), and due to my experience with the students/leaders and their responses, I began to reflect on my task as a teacher and facilitator as a multi-positional practice. In his understanding, people are relationally and dialogically embedded with each other and the outside world. The concept of withness is about being present in our interactions *with* others and sensing openings and possibilities within our communication instead of observing others from a distance. This approach also indicates attention to unfinished and open processes. Shotter emphasises the movement through his concept of thinking in duration. In my experience, it means that I must still be prepared for my teaching and facilitation, but I must also be prepared to meet whatever comes up and therefore act, being both prepared and unprepared at the same time.

## Being part of an organisation again

After a couple of years, I was offered a permanent position at the institute at the University College. In the beginning, I rejected the offer, but the new leaders insisted, and by promising the same kind of freedom, we decided that I should take on part-time employment. Shortly after, it became full-time employment because I found the work at the institute meaningful. Surprisingly, I felt a sense of belonging without too much limitation on my need for freedom. I met new co-workers and a community based on a strong passion for making a difference in the public welfare sector and facilitating learning with the leaders to whom I could strongly relate. I felt both recognised and appreciated for how I contributed to the development of the new institute and accomplished many different tasks with my own passion and strong dedication to my work – a job that I also found myself reasonably competent to do. This feeling of freedom, to contribute in a way that makes sense to both me and to others, I found of great value, and I have found that this felling of belonging and being free at the same time is an ongoing negotiation process.

After a while, I was asked to work on a job, and three other colleagues gave me valuable experience of belonging as a continuing process. However, the teamwork became more and more conflictual, and it became obvious that we thought about leadership and teamwork in very different ways. What I met was a determination to stay in the expert position. The two colleagues believed that relating in a symmetric relation to leaders, working at a top level in municipalities in Denmark, would result in a lack of respect and legitimacy in our own roles as facilitators. They also seemed to find their own roles as leaders of the programme significantly different from the other teachers involved. We talked a lot about it and tried to deal with the differences, and still, it became more and more difficult to find common ground. I felt that I was not respected for my points of view, and I felt that two of the others did not trust my inputs, which they denied. After several discussions, I felt both angry and frustrated because I thought the value of my experience and professional skills were being violated. I remember a car ride home from a session with one of the other team members. She shared my experience of not being acknowledged and respected. We talked a lot, and in the end, we agreed to talk to our own leader about our experiences. This process was unusual for both of us – we both saw ourselves as employees that were able to handle our own conflicts. I remember feeling anxious about including our leader and about whether she would think of me as a problem.

The insights from this conflict were, first of all, that our leader took our experience very seriously. She facilitated several meetings for the group trying to deal with the conflict. She also showed character by underlining how she wanted teams to work together respectfully. I found here a leader and an organisation capable of containing problems and the feelings that came with conflict without this being a problem. In the team, we agreed to disagree on various things, and because of that, the other colleague and I chose to leave the group in the middle of the process. The second consequence of this situation was a strengthened relationship with this one colleague, which has meant a close partnership in our professional lives for several years. It also provided me with an experience about not having to agree with everybody but still remain friendly colleagues, which is the case with both of the others. My sense of belonging was under pressure during this conflict. However, through the process our leader took responsibility to facilitate, I rediscovered a way to feel some belonging without having to adapt or without having to compromise my freedom as an individual too much.

My work at the University College has developed over the years from teaching the leadership programmes to more and more local leadership development programmes in different kinds of organisations in Denmark's public sector. This work is often combined with other development activities than teaching, such as coaching, supervision, facilitation etc. As a group of colleagues working and researching in this field, we always chase new literature and find great inspiration in my collaboration with co-workers. While doing a review on "relational leading" to develop the programme, I began to think that in the social constructionist focus on becoming, we seemed to have forgotten the individual's history and that we might still have to focus on *being*. I got interested in an article by Küpers, who, based on the work of Merleau-Ponty, introduces a concept of be(com)ing (Küpers, 2013). He combines the focus on intrapersonal being and the interpersonal becoming and withdraws the dualism. This article made me think of the social constructionist ideas, and I found that something was missing in the strong focus on language and becoming. When we focus strongly on the spoken language in the process of becoming, we miss out on the rest of the body. Also, being preoccupied with becoming processes does not take our history and who we already have become seriously enough. Further, when focusing on the future becoming, we seem to lose perspective on what is going on in our current practice and how we can learn from that.

For the last couple of years, I have been curious about including these perspectives and combining them with some social constructionist ideas. Here I was introduced to the theory of complex responsive processes (Stacey & Mowles, 2016). Stacey and Mowles write about interaction and not only about the spoken dialogues. They indicate a focus on individuals *in* organisations interacting in complex patterns of predictability and unpredictability. They also take into consideration that human interaction is based on both conscious and unconscious processes. *"A complex responsive processes perspective also draws attention to the unconscious processes in which people are unaware of how they use ideology to justify power relations and patterns of inclusion and exclusion"* (Stacey & Mowles, 2016:428). In my work with leadership development, it becomes central to focus both on the language and the linguistic construction of our identity and take the unconscious and non-articulated processes and power relations into consideration.

In general, I have found a more critical voice towards some of the social constructionist ideas, based on some of Stacey and Mowles´ perspectives, while maintaining a strong orientation towards individuals and the social. Stacey and Mowles state that *"Social constructionists and pragmatists hold that it is impossible to take the position of objective observer and that those who do so are simply ignoring the impact of their own participation or lack of it"* (Stacey & Mowles, 2016:35). A pragmatist approach subscribes to some of the same ideas and seems to be a way to nuance some of the approaches from the social constructionist perspective. The social constructionist perspective loses the paradox between the individual and the social, where only the social counts. The emphasis of discourse and the idea that we can create a more positive world by talking more positively about the future is a relativist position of the social constructivists. From a pragmatist perspective, there is a world "out there" irrespective of our thoughts and feelings about it, which resonates with my critical perspective on the social constructionist ideas. Understanding my own experience of engaging with others is based on taking this engagement seriously.

## Conclusion

Looking back on my P1, I see a strong theme about individuality and sociality. In my childhood, I was fighting to maintain a strong feeling of self while at the same time being governed by the family values and the *Law of Jante*. In my work life, I try to find balances between doing what people expect from me or hire me to do and at the same time doing it with my own best intentions based on the knowledge and the experience I bring with me. The development in demands for working with leadership development in the Danish welfare sector is also changing. Going from offering education for leaders, we develop leadership programmes required by specific organisations demanding specific skills among their leaders. I feel challenged by this change in several ways. First of all, it seems more difficult for me to meet these demands and still be true to my own perceptions of leadership and learning. Again, I find that people in organisations are thought of like instruments or objects. At the same time, I wish to find ways of interacting to try to make an impact to disturb or even change this perspective.

Joining the Doctor of Management Programme is one way to find new ways of working with leadership development. My interest is in working with leadership development with consideration and respect for both the individual and the social power relations we are all part of without degrading people or becoming instrumentalised. Engaging with the DMan community has sharpened my interest in focusing my research on working with leadership practices, considering a dialectical relation between the individual - the social, belonging - freedom and being - becoming. So how can I and others navigate these apparent opposites in our everyday work within the practice of leadership?

# Project 2 - Power relations and identity

## Introduction

A central theme in my work life has been a search to find ways of working within the field of leadership development, based on a nuanced and complex understanding of the people I work with and my interaction with them. In my P1, my attention was brought to the theme of the contradiction between belonging to a community and being accepted by a group on the one hand. On the other, the feeling of freedom to pursue individual ideas and wishes. In this project, I want to inquire into a deeper understanding of these contradictions and the interdependency between the individual and the social and how these interrelations affect my work around leadership development.

The narrative in this project presents an experience in my practice of facilitating leadership development where various patterns of positioning ourselves and others, when interactions in groups appear and how these patterns challenge my understanding of leadership development and my role as a consultant in these processes.

## Narrative - conflict and contradictions

Over the years, I have worked closely together with managers from the social services sector in Denmark. Sophie was a manager I knew well because she had attended one of my educational leadership programmes for this specific sector. In 2018, we held monthly meetings where we reflected together on her job as a manager. One day she contacted me and asked if I would help facilitate a two-day seminar on sector-specific leadership for some of her subordinates. Sector-specific leadership is currently a huge topic in the Danish Welfare sector; it is conceived of as leadership closely connected to the field of work in direct relation to citizens. The field of work in Sophie's organisation is to take care of physically and mentally disabled citizens, who live in public sector homes with 24-hour care. Sophie is the overall manager in this area, and below her are the five managers of the different care homes. There are 2-5 managers at each care home, each responsible for local units and employees. In addition, Sophie is the manager of the shared support staff. The participants at the seminar consisted of all the managers and every member of the centralised support staff, such as HR consultants, financial consultants, and nurses, in total approximately 30 persons. She told me that they only had the budget to have a facilitator for the first day and that she would handle the process herself on the second day. I knew her to be an experienced facilitator, so I did not anticipate any problems, and we agreed that part of my job was to help frame a process for the second day. This work assignment was familiar to me, so I agreed to meet with her, two of her managers, and the HR consultant to talk more about the contents of the seminar.

## The preliminary meetings

At the meeting, Sophie introduced me to the other planning group participants; the two managers Marge and Helen, and the HR consultant Laura and I introduced myself to them. After our presentation, Sophie turned to the new overall policy and strategy.  She said that she wanted the seminar to focus on developing the quality of the services based on the new strategy and my input on sector-specific leadership. It became clear that Helen and Marge were more concerned with the current economic situation, explaining that there had been a major cut in their budgets but that the specific savings had not yet been pointed out. This situation would strongly affect their employees, and it was obvious that they were emotionally affected by the situation. Marge argued that she could not find any more money in her budget and could not agree to firing more staff.

After they had all talked about this for a while, I asked if they were sure that it was a good idea to have the seminar about the new policy and sector-specific leadership at this time. The seminar was supposed to address a new policy, a new strategy, the future budget, and how they would like to work with sector-specific leadership. Listening to the managers, I wondered whether the participants could ignore the budget cuts. Sophie replied that there would never be a good time and that she really wanted the seminar to be held for the two days that they had planned. Since there was still some time until the seminar was to be held, we agreed not to plan the agenda until shortly before it was due, to find out how far in the budget cut process they had come and what kind of process could be facilitated, based on our collective judgement. I remember thinking after the meeting that, as usual, a lot was going on in this organisation and that I was not sure that talking about leadership development in order to increase the quality of the care for the citizens and planning strategic actions for the future would be the most valuable thing for them. However, I waited until the next meeting in order to see what happened next.

More than a month later, we met again, and I found that not much had changed. The money the managers were asked to identify as budget cuts had not been found because Sophie was still negotiating with the management of the municipality. The managers were still frustrated about the situation, but Sophie maintained her belief that the seminar should be held and clearly wanted them to make some kind of progress. Therefore, I tried to think about a process, which addressed what was actually going on in the organisation at that time, combined with a response to the wish for creating some kind of blueprint, focusing on the need for leadership development to carry out the new policy and the new strategy for the area. The blueprint was to plan different kinds of future actions to develop the sector-specific leadership and increase the quality of the care.

I agreed to present different angles on how to think about sector-specific management. Then I suggested an introduction to the complex mechanisms at stake in organisational change combined with a reflection on the emotions based on their current situation. The theme of emotions was my effort to meet some of what seemed to be going on in the organisation, based on the budget cuts. They all agreed, and Helen and Marge found the perspective on emotions especially valuable.

A couple of days after the second meeting, I sent a programme for the two-day seminar and a template for creating the blueprint focusing on individual and collective development initiatives. Sophie commented that they were happy about the process. However, they needed to have exact times on the different items for the days, and I sensed tension from Sophie and the HR consultant, revealing how they wanted to feel in control so that the process could actually turn out the way we planned. I accepted the changes, but it is also my experience that these planned time schedules never tend to last; you cannot totally control these processes, so my impression was that it was a waste of time, but if they found it helpful, it was fine by me. Sophie also sent me her presentation for the beginning of the day to make sure that I knew what she would talk about and could relate to this content to plan my facilitation.

## The seminar

Sophie opened the seminar by presenting the new policy for the specific kind of social sector they work within and thereby the new strategy for the social area in this particular municipality. Afterwards, she spoke about the economic situation, not by talking about the major cutbacks, but by showing the budget for this year and next. She presented them as givens, and there were few questions on her presentation.

After Sophie's presentation, I introduced myself and the programme for the day and immediately continued talking about what elements could be addressed when working with sector-specific leadership. I added that based on this input, every institution and two groups of the support staff should talk about how they wanted to improve the quality of the work in the care homes. The conversation should be based on the policy, the strategy, and the economic conditions that Sophie had presented and inspired by my input. Their reflections were to be shared afterwards in the large group. After lunch, the presentations from each group witnessed many ambitious thoughts and ideas on how they could improve the quality of care. They did not talk about leadership practice but more about what the perfect care home should look like. Expressing dreams in order to be able to follow that path in the future had over the years been a familiar way for us to work together for them to find new leadership practices.  At the same time, I remember thinking to myself that I had heard many of the ideas before at another seminar with some of the same people four years earlier.

The next item of the agenda was a presentation from me about what kind of issues leaders had to deal with when working with change and facilitating learning processes with other people. My main theme was that they were dealing with complex mechanisms and processes in working with the intentions they had presented. I reflected on the importance of taking people's professional identities seriously and how changes might provoke strong emotions. I also emphasised the need to develop a reflexive practice at work during change processes to deal with anxiety.

After a short coffee break, they were asked to create groups across the different departments, reflecting on what kind of complexity they would imagine they might meet or had already met in their task as managers. It was an open topic, and I suggested that it could be about themes such as emotions, values, beliefs, conflicts with themselves or others, but I wanted them to choose the most important theme from their perspective. They all went into groups, but I sensed some kind of tension in the conversations; as I walked around from one group to another, the response to my presence varied from invitations to join the dialogue, ignorance of my presence or silence. I could not quite get a grip of what was at stake here, so I was prepared to be surprised. When we all met again, I invited everybody to share some of the main themes of their dialogues. One of the first comments was that a manager had been talking to one of the consultants from the central support staff. That conversation made the manager realise that she did not have a clear impression of what it was that support staff were doing.

It became clear to me that they had been talking about the imminent cost cuts and that they were primarily concerned about where to find the huge amount of money. More managers talked about the lack of transparency from the support staff, and one addressed the issue that their work was not considered helpful at the care homes.

At one point, I could see one of the HR consultants was about to cry, trying to explain the different tasks involved in her job. Some of the managers raised the criticism of the support staff, and the latter group were then defending themselves. One manager, Bree, said directly that she did not know what the support staff were doing, and the way she saw them, they were more disruptive than helpful. At this point, I stopped them and suggested that they reflect on what was going on in the room. One of the managers said that this was not how they wanted to talk to each other and that it did not contribute positively. It was clear to me that she disliked both the tone and the conversation. Another stated that some of these things had to be said, and I found myself agreeing. I shared that I saw a competition going on, and I asked if that resonated. One of the HR consultants said that she found it quite uncomfortable.  It was hard to always be seen as an unwelcome disturbance when all they wanted was to be helpful.

At some point, Sophie also commented that they could not survive without the support staff, but she was more or less ignored. It seemed that they were not really listening and responding to each other, but it was more like a series of interjections. As the facilitator, I was trying to make them elaborate on the comments to recognise the differences in opinion and the sense-making behind them. From my perspective, this situation was also a chance to get conflicts out in the open and make some of the difficult relationships more transparent for the group, so I kept on opening for reflecting and commenting. The managers also began to criticise each other by arguing that they should not speak to colleagues in such a hostile tone. Again, I raised the question of what they thought was going on in this conversation, and Marge commented that, of course, they were all concerned about their own care home in order to avoid cost savings. Slowly they got quieter and quieter, and I felt they were looking to me to find a way to fix it or escape from the situation. Sophie was surprisingly quiet. She seemed to expect me to be in charge of the situation. Therefore, I ended this process by saying that I thought this was a perfect reflection of what they might also have to deal with in their group of employees at the care homes. My thoughts were that the anxiety they had just experienced might also emerge in their group of employees. Therefore, the last task for the day was to talk about how they would deal with that circumstance in their specific institution.

We had spent more time than planned, so I closed the day by giving a few minutes of reflection on their responsibilities as managers and how to see themselves as role models and reflect on their impact on the daily life at the care homes. This perspective arose from the understanding that if the employees were to change, the managers must change as well. I also reminded them that the day after, they had to work on the blueprint for what actions they would initiate to take their responsibilities seriously. I sensed while talking about these responsibilities that some of the participants felt uncomfortable with the situation. It did not seem that they were listening. I thought that we had not dealt with the conflict as thoroughly as we might have for them to move on afterwards. Looking back, I would have liked to resolve the conflict even though I knew this outcome was not possible, given time constraints.

I was thinking about my responsibility as a consultant. I felt important things had become visible for all of us, but I also did not like to leave them feeling miserable and frustrated. At least I would want them to think that they were moving forward, that they had learned something, so I hoped that by making the conflict visible, they would address their responsibility towards it.

The day was coming to an end, and it seemed that the energy had somehow left the room. Sophie came to me and asked if I could please stay afterwards to help them find a way to move on tomorrow. I felt that she was not happy with the way things had turned out because she seemed uncomfortable and irritated by the conflict that had emerged. I sensed that she had to clean up a mess, and I felt responsible for leaving them like this. She did not respond to me with anything but positive remarks, but still, I turned her frustration towards myself.

After we had finished, Helen, Marge, Laura, Sophie, and I sat down in the corner of the room. Sophie said that she wanted us to discuss how to pick up on things the next morning. Obviously, she did not like as much conflict as we had had on this first day and wished that people would work constructively together, implying that the work reflections on the conflict had not been constructive. I decided that it was not the time to challenge her because they all seemed anxious about the next day, and I sensed the need for harmony. I remember feeling confused about why they made such a big deal out of the different positions and disagreements that had come up. Even though the conversations had been tense, I found that it helped get it out in the open. However, I found myself being concerned about whether they thought I had done my job well enough. They clearly wanted to control the process tightly the day after. I emphasised that I thought it was important not to ignore what had happened that day and the power struggles that had become visible. Laura was very emotionally affected.  She said that she could not handle the managers' critique of the support staff.  It seemed that she just wanted to pretend that the conflict did not exist. She expressed specific anger towards Bree, who, according to Laura, was extremely hostile and the one who was most responsible for the harsh tone. I had been mostly listening. Sophie almost apologised that she wanted to change the programme, but, to me, it seemed natural to change the process as a response and adjustment to what is going on.

On my way home in the car, I was filled with contradictory feelings. First, I was afraid that they did not think I had done my job well enough; I was afraid that they would blame me for the way this conflict had developed and that I could not ensure an environment where everybody was talking politely to each other. Instead, I had encouraged and contributed to a process where people had been hurt and even close to tears. I started to question myself. Did I contribute to making the conflict worse than it was initially; should and could I have closed it down instead of opening up? I also began to think about my mandate to actually invite these people to explore their relationships in the room. They did not seem to like it, and they had not given their consent to participate in such a process. On the contrary, I was there to help them develop their leadership and how they were working together on their common task. The conflicting relations between them had become visible. I was thinking about my DMan programme, where we are encouraged to deal with our experiences attentively and thoughtfully, even if they were anxiety-provoking. I myself did not find the conversation at the seminar very comfortable. However, despite this, I found it important to stay with the conflict that had become visible to find out how the relationship between the managers and the support staff might influence their everyday practice.

By reflecting on what we were experiencing together and dealing with the anxieties in the room, I thought they could learn something. Therefore, I found that I had good arguments for doing as I did, but still, I felt anxiety about the possibility that Sophie and the others did not think that I had done well. The only thing that calmed me was that when I said goodbye, Sophie told me how happy she was that I had been there and that she was unhappy that I should not join them the following day. Even though it was their choice to hire me only for one day, I felt bad about leaving them and not helping them further.

## Initial reflections

Writing and reading my narrative and, through this, reliving my experience clarifies that my engaging with groups of people like this addresses many different themes. First, I chose this narrative because the confusion and insecurity I experienced in my role as a consultant puzzled me. Pursuing my own belief and ambitions while at the same time honouring the acknowledgement of others is important to me, and maybe I did not succeed in doing so on the day of the seminar. Trying to live up to this on the day of the seminar, I felt caught up in contradictory thoughts and feelings about how I engaged with the other participants and questioned the contribution of my work. On the one hand, I found that we momentarily reflected on the relations between the participants and how the differences and even the competition between the groups might influence their working together, which I found could be valuable for them. On the other hand, I felt insecure about my own expectations and the expectations of others in my role as a consultant.

The focus on emotions was part of the plan for the day, but the process of dealing with it and changing the schedule for the day made me unsure of my mandate. As a consultant, I understand my role as a conductor of reflections and dialogues, which enables new realisations or perspectives on the work of the participants, and at the same time felt responsible for the agenda and the schedule that I had negotiated with the small group at the meetings before the seminar. The participants' reactions might have created anxiety in me, including a fear of not being a consultant they found helpful, and I found myself needing their recognition and appreciation. Looking back, I see that I got nothing but appreciation from them, but I still felt stuck in my own sense-making of the experience.

Several times since the seminar, I have asked myself if my decision to spend more time on the conflict that arose was because I found it interesting and necessary to deal with it or if it was the participants' wish as well. I also wonder why I did not spend ´even´ more time on the conflict when I found that it meant something and affected their working together. Experiencing doubt is familiar for me in my practice. I know that if I had chosen a different path, something else might have occurred. However, I am curious about why I was left with these contradictory feelings of being quite satisfied with having stayed with the reflections on an important but difficult issue, which I might have spent even more time on if I had listened to my DMan perspectives and, at the same time, struggling with a sense of inadequacy in my role as a consultant. What were the expectations that I had to meet, and from where did they come? My animating question for this project is why I responded to this process with such contradictory emotions, pressures, and pulls on my identity?

Chris Mowles argues for understanding organisational life as "*…the constant patterning and interweaving of intentions which express power relationships. In any consultancy intervention, the consultant temporarily joins and contributes to this patterning, and will find themselves caught up in what can be very powerful processes*" (2011:51). In this project, I want to explore the power dynamics around the seminar and how competing expectations of my role as a consultant emerge and from which these dynamics originate. I want to inquire into how we respond to each other and interact around leadership development and how the feeling of threat towards my identity might have emerged.


## Power

To explore the contradictions that I found myself caught up in within the narrative, I have become interested in the power dynamics and the power negotiations going on in the process of planning and carrying out the seminar. First, I will draw on some of the work of Michel Foucault and later complement it with another approach from Norbert Elias. Both of these perspectives present understandings of the subtle power mechanisms we are subjected to in our social life, and at the same time, the process of how we are continuingly co-creating the social. To explore my contradictive feelings and the threats to my identity, I find it relevant to explore the power relations in which I got caught up. Power, in Foucault's understanding, is a fundamental force that exists in all relations. As such, he is interested in what power is and how it is played out in relations, focusing on institutional power and discourse. With this perspective, I want to explore how power plays a part in the work around the leadership development seminar in my narrative.

A power perspective reflects upon the dynamics that enable and constrain us in our interactions as participants. My experience on the day of the seminar made me doubt my choices during the day, and I found myself trying to meet different expectations from different stakeholders and myself. The result of this was contradictory feelings and an experience of both being true to and compromising my own judgement at the same time. Therefore, I want to address the power dynamics in the narrative and explore how these affected the interaction and produced doubt and contradictory feelings.

## Foucault on disciplinary power

A common perspective from scholars is to understand power as the direct or indirect exercise of power and focus on observable individuals, objects or incidents (Dahl, 1957, Bachrach & Baratz, 1970). Steven Lukes criticises the focus on direct or indirect power. He introduces a third dimension, where the power is invisible and does not belong to the tradition of understanding power regarding visible conflicts (Lukes, 1974). Michel Foucault can be connected to Lukes' third dimension. However, in contrast to Lukes, Foucault is not interested in the results of power or to localise power. However, he is interested in the relationships of power (Flyvbjerg, 1991:105), which is why I find this perspective interesting with the aim of exploring the more subtle power relations in the narrative.

Michel Foucault was a French philosopher who was interested in how the foundation of modern society emerged. Foucault held a focus on history and a genealogical approach to power. He is interested in techniques and practices of power and focuses on domination and constraints in his perspective on power. He tried to denaturalise the common understandings of truths as he often writes about the excluded discourses, the children, the mentally ill, the "perverts", and the criminals (Heede, 2004). In most of his work, Foucault was interested in power, and his understanding of the concept of power was that it is a productive and creative force. In this way, Foucault does not think of power as something possessed by individuals but rather as being exercised (Foucault, 1979:26)

> *"Power is not an institution, and not a structure; neither is it a certain strength we are endowed with, it is the name that one attributes to a complex strategical situation in a particular society"* (Foucault, 1980:93).

...and further

> *"Power is not something that is acquired, seized or shared, something that one holds on to or allows to slip away"* (Foucault, 1980:94).

He operates with different broad angles on power, and in some of his work, he seems to understand power almost as an agent in itself. Foucault brings attention to institutional power and the mutual relation between power and knowledge. He combines knowledge and power, not in a common-sense understanding that more knowledge creates a powerful position, but by relating knowledge to discourses, which achieve the status of being accepted as truths in a given context. In this way, he describes power as being everywhere, not as an institution, structure or force, that specific people possess, but as a complicated situation in a specific context. The power relations are not explicit in relation to, e.g., economic processes or sexual relations, but must be seen as immanent in these (Foucault, 1994[1976]:99).

As mentioned in my P1, Foucault also focuses on the subject as processes of subjection in power relations. From this perspective, power produces both knowledge and identity. He combines power and subjection, as he understands that we are subjected by power and become subjects through processes of power. He combines power and discourse and in his perception of processes of subjection, he finds it important to understand the positions the discourse makes available for the actions of the subject. Discourses emerge through relational processes of power and occur in our conversations as "true" knowledge. This point is connected to what Foucault calls disciplinary power, where the knowledge on which we base our interactions is produced by the power of discourse (Foucault, 1991).

In my narrative, I see several examples of disciplinary power. We all base our understanding and actions on specific truths, which seem to define the way we interact before and at the seminar. Already at the preliminary meetings, we were caught up in a preoccupation with concepts and expectations as to what would be helpful with which to work. First, the strong focus on sector-specific leadership and the new policy, the strategy, and the budget as concepts we assumed should be prioritised at the seminar. Later in the seminar, we turned to dialogue in smaller groups on intentions for the future and, after that, reflections on the emerging conflict between the participants. Looking back, I can see that we had many different things going on in only one day. From a Foucauldian perspective, this makes me reflect on the dominating discourses in my work and how the power relations might have influenced our way of working on the day of the seminar. My main ambition for my work is for the people I work with to learn something. On the day of the seminar, my work was from my perspective also concerning learning activities. However, what are the dominating discourses on learning that plays a role in this narrative?

## Dominating discourses of learning

Foucault helps me see how knowledge has emerged as dominating truths in my work on the day of the seminar. A cognitivist approach has traditionally influenced the perspectives on learning in the Danish educational sector. Cognitive theories of learning focus on knowledge, perception and thinking, e.g. Piaget (1952[1936]). Focus is on the individual's acquisition of knowledge and skills. As an employee at the University College, the scholastic paradigm of understanding learning as the transmission of knowledge from a teacher to the students is without a doubt still a paradigm that I operate within. In this way, there are clear positions, with the teacher as the knowing part and the unknowing student in need of learning.

Learning theory became slowly connected to organisational research, and the cognitivist ideas were challenged from research that covered theories on decision-making (Cyert & March, 1963, March & Simon, 1958). The studies show how leadership decisions are made; they are not based on knowledge and information and not as rational choices. Instead, this perspective raised the question of how leaders' decision-making can be improved by working with the way they think and how they handle knowledge (Elkjær, 2005).

One critical approach to popular learning theories, which consists of merely individual cognitive processes of communication of knowledge from a sender to a receiver, comes from a social constructionist perspective. This approach introduces a relational understanding of learning as a social process, where knowledge and meaning are co-constructed. The understanding of learning moves away from transferring knowledge to conceptualising learning processes as social processes, e.g., sense-making processes through dialogue (Gergen & Gergen, 2005). From Gergen & Gergen's point of view, learning must also address the fact that education and learning must focus on relational processes as dialogues. Often these dialogues are about wishes for the future because Gergen & Gergen argue that we create the future through conversations (2005).  With this approach, they argue that in contrast to realism, social constructionist ideas work on a meta-level because the focus is to understand people's understandings (Gergen & Gergen, 2005:67)

Other socially oriented theories on learning focus on a combination of knowledge and practice (Lave & Wenger, 1991). They draw attention to the participation in specific communities of practice and argue that learning is about more than acquiring knowledge. They understand learning as situated and played out through legitimate peripheral participation where people understand specific norms and the culture of the community of practice (Lave & Wenger, 1991). Opposite to Gergen, who argues that we create the world through language, Lave and Wenger stress the concept of participation. Stacey & Mowles points out that Wenger explains learning processes in terms of a duality between reification and participation, and they argue for an understanding of paradoxes rather than dualisms (2016:222).

Practice and especially experience are also central for Dewey's pragmatic approach to learning. He integrates the individual and the social by addressing body, mind, thinking and practice while relating these to how phenomena become socially and culturally meaningful (Elkjær, 2005). Dewey emphasises that the experiences we learn from arise when existing habits or understandings fall short, which leaves us with uncertainty and demand for exploration and reflexive thinking. *""We learn by doing because our world is a practical world, which we can only know through action. And our reflexive knowing of this world is necessitated by breakdowns of, and problems with, our activities. If we lived in a world in which our activities were never interrupted, then growth and learning would be impossible"* (Dewey, 1934, as quoted in Brinkmann, 2013:164).

Compared to the social constructionist focus on our language and our understandings and reflections on how we understand the world, Dewey has a broader focus on actions and reflections of our breakdowns in order to learn. The reflexive processes seem to point to the past from a social constructionist perspective. In contrast, Dewey seems to address the need for reflection *in* action when encountering breakdowns, and inherent in his thinking is a stronger focus on the present and the future.

Reconsidering my narrative, I reflect on how all the different learning paradigms I have introduced above seem to exist alongside each other. Even though I do not see myself as a teacher believing in cognitivist ideas of learning, I realise that I am disciplined, positioned, and position myself as an expert. Working at the University College includes me in a strong tradition of teaching, where researchers and professors are hired because of their field of expertise. I also have a history with several of the managers because I have been their teacher at their leadership education. Right from the preliminary meetings when I presented myself, in order to legitimate my role, I pointed out how I knew their organisation and how I had experience in working within sector-specific management. Sophie requested that I give a presentation about how to work with sector-specific leadership, and we all seem to accept that this is one way of legitimising the choice of consultant, and I do take the teaching role.

Inspired by a more social constructionist understanding, I ask the participants to make sense of what I have said about sector-specific leadership and then formulate their visions for the future. The participants wrote their visions on large posters, and by collaborating on this in their local management groups, the intention was that the forming of the future had begun. Even though the focus is on social and more circular learning processes, I experience my thoughts simultaneously based on more linear thinking. I reflect on the fact that I had heard the same visions before and that they had not been realised. This fact indicates a critical approach to the social constructionist approach where expressed visions are central for creating the future and accepting the fact that sometimes the world is deaf to our dreams or expressed visions.

When the reflection on what was going on in the organisation resulted in conflict between the two groups, another learning approaches seem to take over. At this point, I changed the agenda in order to be able to reflect on the current practice and experiences that played out in the discussion. This situation was not only a reflection on their practice, but specifically on the problematic issues about the collaboration between the managers and the support staff as they emerged in the present. My choice to stay with this conflict, to reflect upon what was going on in the present, how the relationship between the managers and the support staff affected the work they had to do together, can be seen as an example of a perspective on learning processes inspired by Dewey, as we were dealing with the present and reflecting in action.

When exploring the disciplining power, I find that several positions seem to be present simultaneously, including elements from all the above-mentioned paradigms of learning. I see that as a consequence, we tried to meet all of the demands arising from the development of these dominating learning discourses. Therefore, over the day, we found ourselves caught up in various understandings of who we were and what we were doing together at different times and in the different situations that emerge.  All the different understandings of learning seem to subject us to the pressure of taking roles as teacher, student, facilitator, visionary management teams, consultant, responsible managers, and produce understandings of different and, to some extent contradictory identities. As I understand the Foucault perspective, this is the very nature of how the relation between power and individual agency can be understood. *"Perhaps the equivocal of the term conduct is one of the best aids for coming to terms with the specificity of power relations. For to conduct is at the same time to 'lead' others (according to mechanisms of coercion which are, to varying degrees, strict)*

*and a way of behaving within a more or less open field of possibilities"*
(Foucault, 1982:220). He points out that there is a close relationship
between power and freedom and states that this requires freedom while
power enables specific actions. *"Power is exercised only over free subjects,
and only insofar as they are free. By this, we mean individual or collective
subjects who are faced with a field of possibilities in which several ways of
behaving, several reactions and diverse components may be realised"*
(Foucault, 1982:221). Foucault almost writes as if power is an agent of its
own, but the way I understand this quote is that he brings attention to the
subjective agency. Trying to live up to all the understandings of my role on
the day of the seminar was also my responsibility and more or less a
conscious choice.

In the narrative, we see different dominating discourses at different times
on the day of the seminar, producing several possible identities. This case
addresses processes of continuing negotiation of the individual identity
among these possibilities. By the role you are invited to and choose to take,
you become who you are. How do we navigate the various possibilities of
forming ourselves when the role(s) you take is(are) not unilaterally defined?
It seems that Foucault addresses the power dynamics that provides a field of
opportunities for individual identity-making but does not address an
individual agency in order to choose your own way to behave or react. So,
when knowledge gets extended and different discourses are simply
accumulated into a more complex pattern, is it possible to break free from
the power that both enables and constrains us to step out of the
discourse(s)?

Foucault offers a view on the overall discursive power mechanisms that
form identities from an archaeological and genealogical perspective.
However, he does not pay much attention to the power relations between

individuals or the smaller groups. Therefore, I would like to bring in Norbert Elias's perspective to supplement Foucault's perspective on power to further explore the power dynamics in the narrative. With this approach, I aim to be able to further understand the experiences in the narrative. From Elias's perspective on power, I will explore further the relationship between the individual and the social and the struggles in which we are embedded.

Power relations and processes of inclusion and exclusion in leadership and leadership development

A complementary way to understand the power in the narrative is presented by the German sociologist Norbert Elias. Elias studied civilisation processes and argues that power forms an integral element of all human relationships (1970). Like Foucault, he does not think of power as something individuals have but introduces a relational perspective on power.

> *"Power is not an amulet possessed by one person and not by another; it is a structural characteristic of human relationships – of all human relationships"* (1970:70).

According to Stacey, Norbert Elias' understanding of power is closely connected to his understanding that social group processes are based on the argument that *"social evolution is a self-organised process of emergent change in patterns of relationship"* (Stacey, 2003:56). Elias states that, *"As the moves of interdependent players intertwine, no single player nor any group of players acting alone can determine the course of the game, no matter how powerful they may be"* (1970:146). In his studies of these interdependencies, he states that it is a central need for all people to belong to a group, and he inquires into how humans connect with each other. The membership in different groups is negotiated as processes of inclusion and exclusion. The mutual dependency between the people being included in a group forms a specific set of social norms (1970). These norms create the structure for developing a we-identity that can only be understood as inseparable from the I-identity. Our belonging to a group is in this way simultaneously forming our I-identity, while at the same time our I-identity is forming the we-identity. In order to understand how these local groups affect our identity, Elias presents a game metaphor. He understands the group members as game players, who play by and develop a specific set of rules, which members have to comply with to be included in the group. The game is continuingly developed, and new power relations emerge (1970:68-71).

One of the most visible power struggles on the day of the seminar was between the managers and the support staff. There was a powerful them/us dynamic between the managers and the support staff. It seemed like the support staff were fighting to be included as legitimate participants in the overall department. In connection with inclusion and exclusion processes, the educational background of the managers plays a significant part. They all have a pedagogical background and have worked in their professional area in the same or other institutions, close to the disabled citizens. The support staff, including Sophie, have different educational backgrounds – as nurses, political scientists, economists, or HR. At the same time, they have never been part of the everyday life at the institutions like those with whom they are aiming to cooperate.

This situation could have created differences in their approach to how they were thinking of themselves and others, which might have led to the divided understanding. Ludwik Fleck (1979) introduces a perspective on thought collectives, where he is paying attention to the different sciences and their specific thought styles. For example, pedagogical science is based on social and humanistic thinking, whereas economics might be based on approaches that claim to be more rational.  Research and knowledge are based on these different thought styles, and Fleck pays attention to the fact that the world cannot be perceived or understood from an objective observer position (1979:120). This perspective can be closely connected to what Foucault calls "episteme". Foucault also has a deep interest in knowledge and the creation of hegemony through different kinds of knowledge. Fleck argues that different research disciplines form collectives around different world views. All the managers are pedagogically educated, and all work as decentralised managers, which might indicate that they could be perceived as a thought collective. The support staff have several educational backgrounds, and only a few are not pedagogues. One of the support staff members, whom I knew well before the day of the seminar, was surprisingly silent during the conversations in the large group. I remember thinking that it was unusual for her but did not think much about the reason. Looking back now, I see that she might be the only person among the support staff who was pedagogically educated and had a history of being a former manager of a local care home. She might have been torn between her loyalty to the thought collective as a pedagogue and her loyalty to the support staff. A sense of belonging to both groups, and an I-identity formed by both we-identities, might have put pressure on her to differentiate from belonging to either group.

Relating further to Elias's ideas, I see one strong group of leaders allying against the support staff. By sharing the same background and sharing the same function as managers, they might have a strong feeling of we-identity. The support staff consists of several different professions, e.g. nurses and economists, and represent different thought collectives, but were seen as one group from the managers' perspective. Their reactions were different, and it did not seem that they had the same feeling of cohesion and feeling of being a group as the managers thought of them. Most of them were very quiet during the conflict: Laura shared her frustration over the comments, some of their facial expressions showed sadness and frustration, and again others did not seem to care. This example might illustrate a stronger we-identity among the managers than among the support staff or a diverse way of responding and emotional reaction.

Sophie, also not being pedagogically educated, might also have been seen as belonging more to the support staff group and not as part of the same thought collective as the managers. The fact that Sophie has the last word in identifying the units to cut their budgets might have created anxiety between the managers. The focus on the budget cuts and the fight for holding on to the resources might have fanned the flames of a more general lack of cohesion between groups in the Danish welfare sector. In general, there is a huge debate in Denmark about the debureaucratisation of the public sector. One of the results of New Public Management has been presented as a significant increase in the number of employees working as support staff. In the political debate, they have been named *the cold hands* in this debate, opposite to the warm hands working directly with the citizens.

The expression of conflict seemed to address a fight for the legitimacy of staff functions in the department because of a fight over resources. The closest leadership reference for the support staff is to Sophie, and they share their office facilities. In contrast, there are two managerial levels in the institutions, located at different addresses. The distance in their everyday practice was in part a physical distance and resulted in a lack of understanding and acknowledgement of each other, which became a central theme of the seminar. It was expressed as a competition over resources and a stuckness towards each other's understandings of their task.

The competitive pattern did not show only between the support staff and the institutions. In addition, there were signs of competition between the institutions. Even though I tried to mix the groups, I found that every institution was preoccupied with its own units. They did not show any kind of thinking or understanding for the department as a whole. It indicates that belonging to different groups can be seen as a competition in itself, and the power is played out between groups. Belonging to different groups might lead to negotiations of which group you feel the stronger belonging to, and therefore which game rules should be prioritised before the others. Belonging to different groups does not necessarily create competition. However, the situation sharpened the hostile environment with budget cuts and uncertainty over the consequences of the changes in the economy as a fight over resources and even a fight for survival.

Simultaneously I found myself in the processes of negotiating my loyalty to different groups. How could I stay loyal to both the managers, the support staff, Sophie, and my own way of thinking like a professional? I did not want any of them to think of me as not recognising their perspectives and wishes, as I was afraid that they would not think of me as a helpful consultant in either one of their views. I see now that I was seeking recognition to avoid exclusion while deciding how to handle the situation. First, I wanted to act responsibly by taking seriously that conflicting opinions and strong emotions had emerged. I wished for the participants to find my facilitation of the conversation helpful and valuable. At the same time, I felt committed to the agreements we had before the seminar and had made in the smaller group about the process of the day. I have worked with this organisation for many years, and it has somehow become part of my professional identity at the

University College, that this organisation is "my" client, and I feel closely connected with the managers who I know well and am deeply interested in what is going on for them. I did not think of it at the time. However, if they did not find my consultancy work helpful, this would also mean that I did not belong with them in the same way anymore, so the fear of being excluded and losing a part of my professional identity might also have affected me.

Looking back, I see now that the fact that Sophie was the top manager present, and that she was the one who hired me for the task and probably would also be responsible for hiring me back later, created a certain kind of relationship with her. As she, late on the day of the seminar, expressed how happy she was that I had been there with her, I felt recognised as her working partner and somehow relieved that she did not blame me for creating a mess. I felt included in her managerial responsibility.

For quite some time, I have had monthly conversations with Sophie to reflect on her leadership practice. We had formed a close alliance and an interdependency between us. The obligations I felt came with this relationship constrained my understanding of my opportunities to respond to what emerged by skipping the agenda to take the experience of conflict seriously. At the same time, I felt a lot of trust in my judgements from Sophie, which might have enabled me to act differently from what we had agreed on before the seminar. It did not seem possible to change the wish for blueprints or respond to what emerged with a total change in the programme. As a guest trying to be included in their organisation, I see now that I did not even suggest this opportunity to Sophie or the participants. However, sensing that this would have been the better thing to do, this then resulted in me questioning my own efforts afterwards.

My belonging to the University College also might have affected me in other ways. The professional game we employees are playing has seemed to be changing in recent times. Earlier, we talked about students and about learning processes. We still do that, but more and more, we talk about clients and customers and facilitating the implementation of organisational change. From a Foucault perspective, it seems necessary to state that nobody is doing it to us (disciplining) but understanding the power dynamics as something we do to each other. Even though I have found myself being critical towards understanding ourselves as suppliers to our clients, I realise that this new discourse might have disciplined me in my working within leadership development. The "client-discourse" subjects me as a supplier, and I find in my narrative that this makes me deliver more of what is demanded from the client than in my earlier understanding of my work, where the focus was more on the facilitation of reflection and learning. This approach also introduces a focus on customer satisfaction and economic turnover. Since the game at my workplace is changing, I have to somehow find my way if I want to still be included there, which might also affect how I think of my role and my relation to the participants on the day of the seminar.

In Foucault's understanding of discourse, power and resistance are connected as a productive opening for change. Vivien Burr states, *"In fact, power and resistance is another ''pair' ' that always go together for Foucault. Prevailing discourses are always under threat from alternatives, which can dislodge them from their position as "truth". … This opens up for people at least the possibility of change through resistance"* (1995:70-71). From this perspective, I wonder if we have been caught up in adapting to the new "client-discourse" while still trying to resist it at the same time when planning the seminar. Trying to act in this fluid understanding of my role as a consultant made me both meet the client's demands of structuring the day and trying to control the process, and at the same time challenge them by changing the agenda, spending more time on the themes that seemed important.

My relation to one of the thought collectives I belong to also affected my actions at the seminar. Being part of the Doctor of Management community has affected my thinking about my own practice. In this community, we work reflexively with our own experiences. Reflecting and talking openly about our experiences and especially addressing difficulties and conflicts to move on with our work has already become central to how I also think about other people´s learning and development processes. Dealing with differences in opinion and conflict had become a part of my way of thinking. As I have experienced these processes in the DMan community, I wanted to include them in my practice. Engaging in patterns with others present both physically and embedded in our identities underlines the complexity of processes in groups like at the seminar.

Therefore, I insisted on staying with the conflict longer than the agenda would leave room for and longer than I might have done before the DMan. I had a feeling of satisfaction with this on my way home. However, I could have encouraged them to explore conflict, even more, I could have gone all the way and shared with Sophie, and maybe others, my ideas and thoughts on how to respond to the conflict in a way that, in my opinion, took the conflicts more seriously and would be more helpful for them. Instead, I found myself disciplined by all these affiliations and found myself partly alienated because I compromised with different aspects of my identity to meet other demands such as client satisfaction. In this way, power struggles were carried out between all of us, that is those who participated on the day of the seminar, and inside of me in the sense of how I relate to the various communities to which I belong.

This perspective raises questions about to what and whom I belong and to whom am I obliged? In addition, how can one deal with belonging and being obliged to several groups or communities at the same time? Elias emphasises the importance of a paradoxical understanding of the individual and the social:

> *"And this fact, that each 'I' is irrevocably embedded in a 'we', finally makes it clear, why the intermeshing of the actions, plans and purposes of many 'I's constantly gives rise to something which has not been planned, intended, or created by any individual"* (Elias, 1991:62).

According to this quote, we are both forming groups and formed by them simultaneously. However, by working with a detailed agenda for a seminar, as a consultant, we are co-producing expectations to a process that no individual can plan or control. Further, working with detailed agendas might create an expectation of me as a consultant that it is my job to manage this predicted process. The word facilitator, which we often use, also indicates an ability or responsibility to make the planned process happen or make it easy. According to Elias' perspective, no single individual can be responsible for what arises in the local interaction. However, through power relations, mutual expectations of the others and ourselves emerge, and thereby we have a collective impact and a shared responsibility. As such, it would have been possible for me, as a consultant, to move on to the next item of the agenda earlier and follow the schedule, but even when I did so later on, the conversations did not stop. On the following exercise and after the end of the programme, the conflict continued more or less explicitly to be part of the conversations in the seminar. In this way, the pattern that emerged in the plenary conversation, based on what the participants were disturbed about, continued afterwards, and the seeds have probably been there before that. Suppose the understanding of different power relations creates a complex pattern from which people continuously develop identity. How does this relate to the way of engaging in activities about leadership development and learning?

## Complex power relations and leadership and consultancy practice

One of the scholars who developed the complex responsive processes theory, Douglas Griffin, compares different understandings about self-organisation that I have found helpful when thinking about organisational processes, which cannot be predicted. He describes systemic self-organisation as the dominant understanding of organisational life. Trying to make sense of what is going on in organisations, Griffin argues that we tend to *"slide automatically into talking about the system as having intention and being ethically responsible"* (2002:2). He criticises the strong focus on the individual, both on the autonomous subject as external observer and on the system as the object. Griffin connects this with systemic self-organisation. A strong belief in an individualised perspective creates a focus on the leader. This perspective can easily cause a heroic understanding of the leader and exaggerated expectations of the skills of the leader in the perspective where no one person can control the organisational processes.

In the narrative, this enables the participants to blame each other, both in the discussion of who does the more meaningful job and later in the reflections on the conflict, where Bree was blamed for creating a hostile environment. At the same time, I take on the individual responsibility of navigating between different expectations and finding my own way of responding to what emerges instead of sharing my reflections and negotiating how to move on together. Afterwards, I felt guilty because of my actions and leaving them without contributing to solving their conflict. In the narrative, the intense focus on the individual becomes visible in how we as participants tend to impose responsibility on ourselves or each other, rather than also understanding the individual actions as formed by relationships. To me, this point is an encouragement to maintain a preoccupation with the individual agency while including the paradoxical approach, which does not leave us without individual responsibility. However, it creates an understanding that we are both being enabled and constrained while in our interactions, we are enabling and constraining others. This debate means a showdown with the dualistic thinking of the individual and the social.

Even when reading theories about relational leadership broadly, there seems to be an overall tendency to adopt dualism in thinking about the relationship between the individual and social perspective. One group of theories emphasises the role of individual history, experience, and values. There seem to be an argument for less of a focus on an individual skillset favouring developing the individual mindset from the perspective of, e.g. a body phenomenological perspective (Küpers, 2013, Slife & Richardson, 2011, Ladkin, 2008, etc.). Another group emphasises the social processes by addressing power relations as a central element in understanding leadership and leadership development and, therefore, addresses cultural norms and discourses as essential in the emergence of leadership (Carrol & Nicholson, 2014). Even though most of these authors seem to argue for the importance of uniting the two perspectives when working with leadership development, they seem to maintain the dualistic understanding. By emphasising that the preferred perspective must be supplemented with the other to capture the complexity, the quest for simultaneity between the two must be considered reinforcing the dichotomy. According to Kennedy, Carrol & Francoeur, drawing attention to this calls for a focus on leaders' ways of relating to the context instead of working with individual leadership skills (2013). Even though these different perspectives seem to demand a fusion between the individual and the social aspects of leadership development, they still maintain a dichotomist approach.

Griffin argues for a transcendence of the dichotomy between individual and social. He states that the thinking of the individual as the *"both...and"* makes *us lose the tension between the individuals as the condition for the possibility of the group and the group as the condition for the possibility of the individuals, at the same time"* (2002:10). As an alternative, he introduces the understanding of the participatory self-organisation as processes *"of interactive participation between self-conscious embodied subjects who are observers and participants, subjects and objects at the same time"* (2002:10). In this way, there is an acceptance of paradoxes. When reflecting on leadership, Griffin argues: *"I move away from this concept of the autonomous individual and develop an understanding of experience as the paradoxical movement of self-organisation which is the living present.* (2002:126). With Griffin's understanding that self-organisation *is* participation, we might know the intentions behind our actions, but we cannot assume that we can predict the outcome. In this way, the idea of implementing or controlling a process becomes an illusion. Focusing on effect or outcome must require that we continuously deal with what is actually going on. He introduces an understanding of the living present as influenced by the individual's past and our intended future. He combines the individual perspective with the emergence of overall patterns in local interaction between the individual agents.

The understanding of a helpful consultant can change over time, which seems to be the case in my narrative. My past with some of the participants and our relationship as teacher and student changed as I was invited to facilitate a seminar, to which they had very specific expectations. During the seminar, the understanding of good facilitation as controlling an agenda and a development plan was challenged by the conflict that emerged in the group. Taking the role of a consultant is one thing, but the way I choose to navigate and form this role while others continuously form others is another. Individual choices are made in dialectical interaction with the social. We are embedded in our social relations but are also responsible for the forming of these relations.

With the understanding of Griffin's participatory self-organisation as an opposite to the systemic self-organisation, he states that we have "moved away from the notion of the autonomous individual but, nevertheless, retained a notion of individuality as emerging in social interaction without appealing to any whole outside of that action" (Griffin, 2002:132). When working with leadership and consultancy, we must understand ourselves as social selves.

Mowles also dissociates from the thinking of the consultant or leader standing outside the organisational system. Mowles argues that *"the dominant theory of consultancy or managerial intervention in organisations is based on systems dynamics where there is an assumption both that an organisation is a self-regulating system and that the consultant/manager is a detached, objective observer who can intervene to help staff bring about specific and necessary change"* (Mowles, 2011:31). I recognise the persuasiveness of this argument as I reflect on my narrative, as my task was that I should help them plan their development of sector-specific management. As I was writing this narrative, I arranged to have a conversation with Sophie about the experiences from the first day, and two of her comments struck me. First, she said that she was happy that I was there with her on the first day of the seminar to experience myself what she was dealing with every day. I felt recognised, I was happy about the kind of relation she expressed, and I was satisfied to get some kind of acknowledgement that my presence might have been helpful to her. Secondly, I see now that both managers and consultants are tangled up in power relations in their work and should not be seen as detached observers. Mowles emphasises the mutual influence between the consultant and the organisation:

> "They are liable to come into an organisation where the patterning of people´s actions and intentions have developed over many years to constrain powerfully what it is possible to say and do, both for employees in that organisation and for consultants. The consultant will offer different ways of understanding these phenomena, but their ability to influence those they are working with will depend on their ability to play the game in which they find themselves caught up. Rather than merely affecting the organisation into which they have been invited, consultants are themselves likely to be heavily affected" (Mowles, 2011:46).

Further, Mowles argues that the consultant brings a temporary form of leadership into the organisation (2009:291). By taking part in the power relations, a temporary "new" leader might interact in different ways, which might help the permanent staff members to new understandings of themselves and each other and to interact in different ways. According to Mowles, this addresses an ethical duty for consultants when they engage in different kinds of power relations (2009). He argues for the need for a strong sense of self for the consultants *"in order to come to terms with how they might exercise leadership ethically … while not getting drawn into manipulation"* (2009:292).


## Summing up

My exploration of power dynamics in this project draws my attention to how power relations are played out when entering organisations or groups, and no one can avoid becoming part of them. From a Foucault perspective, we are disciplined by overall discourses of various kinds, from which knowledge arises. The discourses have helped me see different identity formations in the narrative and how I was subjected to these as a consultant on the day of the seminar. With Elias's understanding, we get included in playing games with rules, which we take part in defining. Entering into organisations and belonging to different groups, both present and not present, means entering power relations that create different and sometimes conflicting understandings and expectations of me as a professional.

In this project, I have inquired into the power relations I were caught up in as a facilitator of a one-day leadership seminar. I see now that my experience of contradictive feelings after the seminar might have been influenced by the power dynamics in which I was caught up. The fact that I did not follow the agenda but decided to spend time on an emerging conflict might have disrupted the dominating ideas of learning and leadership development, making me question the legitimacy of my actions. I did not do as we had planned because I believed that this was not what was needed. We did not know what would emerge on the day of the seminar. When unexpected and even difficult situations emerge in organisations, consultants or leaders should stay with it to facilitate change.

Instead, in this narrative, I see a dominating understanding of creating visions for the future, which does not seem to take conflicts seriously to enable us to learn and change but rather create room for avoiding conflict. I see how in my actions I challenged my own earlier perceptions of a facilitator's work and how I challenged my own former identity inspired by a social constructionist perspective and maybe also the participants' experience of a consultant. I also challenged the dominant understanding of the consultant and how we at the University College should engage with clients.  Simultaneously, the feelings of personal guilt I experienced on my way home might have been reinforced because of the blame game between the participants, by which I was affected.

In this narrative, my argument is that the power relations and identity formation must be understood from a dialectical perspective on the individual and the social. I see that the current social relations on the day of the seminar and the power relations from belonging to other groups are played out. However, my argument is that also challenging old ashes from former communities to which I belonged, in this case a strong sense of belonging to a social constructionist group, might provoke anxiety and contradictory feelings.

I see now how I was negotiating my identity at the one-day seminar to meet various, and at some points, opposing expectations. One result was an ambitious attempt to meet many of the expectations from others and myself. I agreed to facilitate a one-day seminar addressing a new policy, a new strategy, a new perspective on leadership, and sense-making in a local context under huge economic pressure. Simultaneously I wanted to take the emerging conflict seriously, while still not leaving the visionary forming of the future. This experience makes me wonder why we try to do and accomplish so much in so little time?

My reflection raises the question of what the consultant entering organisations is to do and how to find out what to do along the way when unexpected things emerge. Being a good leader or a good consultant, I must understand the power relations I become part of when I step into a new assignment. I have to find the courage to challenge what I get caught up in. This narrative is an example of trying to live up to expectations from too many social communities at the same time that might very well leave us with doubt and contradictive feelings about our efforts. I see that this calls for a reflexive praxis in my work as a consultant to make continuingly new judgements when power dynamics and new and unexpected situations emerge.

According to Mowles, this kind of judgement calls for a strong sense of self. He argues that *"a developed sense of self enables consultants paradoxically, a fuller exchange with the other"* (2009:292). Negotiating identity in power relations then seems to call for a strong sense of self to reflect on what power relations I get caught up in and on my efforts to challenge dominating existing beliefs when needed. Thus, when understanding the individual and the social as paradoxically connected, what does it mean to have a strong sense of self? How do we work on this? These questions are my entrance to project 3, where I will explore these themes further.

# Project 3 Sense of self and others - visibility and invisibility

## Introduction

In my P2, I explore how power plays a part in the making of my identity as a professional when trying to live up to different contradictive expectations.

My argument was that entering into organisations means encountering different complex power relations. All participants relate to different groups, both those immediately present and the groups in which we are historically and culturally embedded. Belonging to different groups creates a complex set of expectations and the informal rules that every individual is formed by and is at the same time forming.

Influenced by my P2, in my understanding power is not something one can possess but an ongoing interdependent process between people on both a micro level with specific people and a macro level, where hegemonic discourses and overall group norms have a strong and powerful influence on our identity. The negotiation processes of power that come with belonging to different groups can lead to pressures and pulls on identity to understand and find ways between different roles, e.g. a teacher, consultant, or learning facilitator. Simultaneously, I found that challenging these dominating discourses that produce knowledge, or even to some extent dissociating myself from the culturally adapted truths, might provoke fear of exclusion and anxiety in the emergence of a new identity.

Negotiating identity in different power relations seems to call for a strong sense of self to hold on to some degree of freedom as an individual and an ongoing reflection of what kind of power relations one gets caught up in, as suggested by Mowles (2009:292). This work addresses the relationship between individual agency and the social disciplining in which selves emerge. The argument from P2 emphasises the importance of paying attention to the processes of negotiation of identity. I am arguing that one must not lose the understanding of the individual and the social as paradoxically interwoven.

In this project, I will explore the understanding of the strong sense of self in processes of negotiating identity. My choice of narrative for this inquiry is partly inspired by my reflections about my participation in the wider DMan community. Since joining the DMan, I have found myself unusually quiet at the community meetings. Every morning at the residentials, we have a community meeting for one and a half hours with no agenda. Inspired by group analysis practice, we sit in a large circle. Both faculty members and students are encouraged to speak about their reflections on what is going on between people in the group. Anxiety provoking themes tend to continually emerge, e.g. the question of being good enough to finish the doctorate.

We also discuss what patterns seem to emerge in our group and how we respond to each other, drawing parallels to organisational life from our shared experiences, where relevant.  I do not usually tend to have problems forming or articulating strong opinions at work. However, in this particular setting, I have found myself not having much to contribute. Even though rationally, I have found the shared reflections both meaningful and necessary in our working together, I have been puzzled about my more silent behaviour at these meetings. I have found that the themes we usually talk about at the community meetings relate to the students' strong emotional reactions. I have seen a pattern where I am perfectly comfortable with other people discussing their strong emotions and problematic experiences with other people. However, paying attention to my own emotions, and being the centre of emotional drama, is something I primarily do in my silent conversations with myself or with selected close friends or colleagues.

In hindsight, I see that the idea of my feelings of anxiety being of any interest to other people seems somehow unfamiliar to me. I recognise this way of relating to my emotions from my childhood, where I learned not to put myself and my emotions in the middle of people's attention, and now realise this ongoing pattern of behaviour in my everyday interactions in my work life as well. Therefore, I have chosen a narrative for my P3, which focuses on my own reactions to an everyday job situation to challenge my own described pattern. The narrative puts me and my experience of self at the centre of my reflections, which earlier would have been a highly unusual narrative for me to choose.

The following narrative has also been chosen because it represents a breakdown in my understanding of my own way of responding in my everyday work life. The theme is about how freedom in my job tends to leave me with too heavy a workload and how a seemingly ordinary and everyday matter of reducing many assignments turned into a crisis of identity.

Narrative – feelings of invisibility
The University College I work for was going through a merger with the other University College in Copenhagen. The process until the merger resulted in several redundancies and voluntary dismissals for a group of my former managers and close colleagues. Simultaneously, the merger meant we had

many new co-workers in our joint department. Managers from the other University College occupied the managerial positions at the two hierarchical levels above my direct manager. Despite this situation and the uncertainty of future structures in the University College, we seemed to move on doing our jobs, more or less in the same way as we used to. To me, this meant taking part in - and being responsible for - many different tasks, both internally and externally, with our clients.

The following narrative took place in a period when the content of my job had changed. For several years, project management of and teaching a tailor-made leadership educational programme in a large Danish welfare organisation had been a significant part of my job. After the end of this educational programme in 2016 I had recently been busy working on various projects, and this narrative begins when I realised that I had far too much work and too little time.


## The meeting with my manager

As a result of the heavy workload, I asked my manager, Grace, to discuss my job assignments. We have had this kind of conversation a couple of times before, resulting from me taking on too many assignments. Based on my earlier experience, I expected our meeting to result in a mutual decision about which projects or assignments to prioritise and which we should leave for other colleagues. It was unusual for me to ask for this kind of help, but I found myself unable to deselect any of my assignments. In our meeting, I gave Grace an overview of what I was currently working on and what assignments I had agreed to take on over the next semester. I presented every task with a story of why it had become important that I was the one who had been assigned to this and how all these reasons have made it difficult for me to delegate to my colleagues. My relationship with Grace has been built on trust and, to a great extent, on self-management. She was rarely included in my considerations and efforts to solve the tasks unless there were challenges in my different work relationships with which she could help me. Looking back, I see now how this kind of leadership has been very important to me. I strongly value the freedom to make my own judgements about my work. Simultaneously these distributed responsibilities and Grace's confidence in my professionalism made me feel recognised.

She shared my view on the difficulties in delegating my assignments but agreed that I was involved in too many things. Her answer was, therefore, that I should not teach in our leadership programme. My stomach tightened, and I felt as if I was under pressure or attack, which made me try to defend my dislike of the suggested solution. I found myself arguing that I had not been teaching for a while and that my work with the students was something I loved. I told her that I felt obligated to the former colleague I had promised to work with experimentally in teaching on a particular course.

Secondly, to verify my judgement, I shared my reflections on how the development of our revised leadership education programme would demand current experience with the students and the courses. This argument was based on a strong wish to include the students' voices and a more political approach about having the kind of arguments I knew could be the more dominant ones in the discussions with my colleagues. I expected to face several disagreements when we revised our programme both in curriculum matters and the didactic approach to the different courses. When changing the content of the education, different teachers usually have very strong feelings about certain literature and others have certain preferences about the way they like to teach. Both Grace and I were also very keen to develop the programme according to our own beliefs. We usually agreed on most issues concerning the educational programme and often fought on the same side. My reason for explaining to Grace that I was preparing solid arguments and that the direct and latest interaction with our students would contribute to a stronger and more legitimate argument in the discussions ahead was, therefore, to convince her that it was a bad idea to let go of my teaching commitment. Acting politically in this way was not unfamiliar in my cooperation with Grace, which might have been why I presented this kind of argument. I felt that to stop teaching the programme would make my voice less significant and powerful in the group. However, the fear of my voice not being recognised as important and, therefore, not having my clear fingerprint on future leadership education was not something I shared directly with Grace. In hindsight, I see that this would bring my individual needs to the centre of our conversation, which would be unusual and probably not acceptable in my thinking.

Grace smiled at me with a sense of resignation. She told me that I would have very strong arguments about why this was not a possible solution no matter what she would suggest. She, therefore, decided for me, something she had rarely done, to cut back on my teaching commitments. Looking back, I am not sure what I had expected. I knew she was right about my unwillingness to let go of my assignments, and still, I felt strongly about teaching this specific course because of the reasons above.  Since she stood firm on her decision and could not find any alternative, I agreed to find out how to do this.

After the meeting with Grace, I found myself stubbornly not wanting to let go of the course. When I had to phone my colleague to tell her about the decision, I found that I simply could not tell her that she was on her own. It was an embodied experience of not carrying out what Grace decided and what I had agreed to, and I felt prevented from being loyal to Grace´s decision. Therefore, I negotiated with my teaching companion that we would still, to some extent, teach together but that she would do a larger amount of the teaching without me. In this way, I compromised on my own wish for more time to spend on my other projects and only half complied with Grace's decision, but I would not have to let anyone down. When I told Grace about my decision to hold on to part of my teaching assignment, she accepted this.

In hindsight, I see that I often feel a huge commitment to most of my tasks and the people involved in them. I recognise a pattern of wanting to be included in many things and a sense of reassurance of my worth through this acceptance. Simultaneously, I am sometimes hesitant to accept larger assignments, which might exclude me from taking on other new tasks. Earlier on, Grace had asked me whether I would like a senior management position in the future. I have always rejected the idea, but as my supervisor at the DMan started to ask me the same questions, I see now that it seems to be difficult for me to decide on assignments or positions that might close future doors for me and, in my opinion, reduce my sense of freedom.

A few months went by, and I kept working on many different kinds of assignments. The merger of the two University Colleges resulted in another process of adjusting and developing the leadership education. Both University Colleges had offered the same Leadership degree, and the task was now to co-create a joint programme. My work involved participation in several internal development processes resulting from the merger, and still, I did my teaching, the different consultancy jobs and worked on my PhD. I decided what invitations or requests I wanted to accept or turn down, although I accepted most of them because I wanted to be included and contribute. I did not like to turn people down, and I also felt recognised when both co-workers and clients invited me. Trying to do my job with the many various tasks I had wanted to work with, I still felt more and more dissatisfied with my work life. At the same time, I blamed myself for feeling this way because I seemed to have had things my way, and still, it was not what I wanted. Burdened with guilt because of my dissatisfaction, I just kept working and decided to wait and see.

Meanwhile, Grace temporarily took another management position because of the merger, and for a period, one of my close colleagues, Sally, took over Grace´s leadership position. In this period, all managers at the University College were to call all employees to an extra one-to-one dialogue about their well-being, so Sally set up a conversation date.


## The employee development dialogue

Looking back, I realise that I had ignored the agreement to reduce my workload. I found that I still felt somehow dissatisfied in my organisational life, and I was still trying to make sense of the cause of my failure to thrive. On several occasions, I had felt ignored by my managers and colleagues. When I heard the new managers from the other University College talk about the strategy and the future for the *new* University College, I found myself irritated since they talked as if they did not know what we had been doing for the last several years, which they probably did not, but also did not bother to ask us. Parallel to this process, I had not been invited into any of the new assignments in the department, which altogether made me feel insignificant and invisible.  Rationally I was able to make sense of the situation. The new managers did not know who we were and what we had worked on, and I knew that both Grace and Sally were trying to protect me from having too much to do. Still, I did not feel as recognised, significant or appreciated as I used to. I had felt the recognition from Grace in the way she trusted me with the freedom to make my own choices, and in my everyday work, I felt a strong bond to the students and the people I worked with, so I did not quite understand my reactions. I could not make sense of my situation, so I acknowledged my feeling of being invisible without knowing the exact reason this feeling occurred but needed to share this feeling with Sally.

As I opened the one to one conversation with Sally, I shared how I did not feel I had any important responsibilities or large projects anymore and did not feel recognised. We talked about my involvement in several ongoing projects, and I realised that I missed having my own projects instead of being invited into everybody else's. I heard myself telling her that not having project management or large responsibilities of my own had made me feel invisible. Sally smiled and showed me her preparation papers for our conversation, where she had written that from her perspective, I had come to be on the edge of the organisation and how she missed working more closely with me. We made sense of my feelings by blaming the lack of larger assignments, and we agreed that we should help each other find another large assignment for me, even though we both knew that this was not a solution we could find overnight. I left the conversation still dissatisfied but recognised by Sally.

Looking back, I realise that we were trying to find a way to "fix" my feeling of invisibility by rationally planning how to make me thrive again. However, we agreed that the circumstances were not changeable at that time but that we had to wait and see. At the same time, we had agreed that her being the temporary manager would not change our close and trust-based relationship. I am sure neither of us wanted to do anything to risk that, so in hindsight, I see now that all we did in this conversation was to agree and postpone any kind of concrete action. I believe that having this conversation with Sally and her resonating with my experience encouraged me to move on even though I did not know what to do to thrive again.

Not long after my conversation with Sally, Grace returned as my manager. She wanted to organise a group of employees, who should be the lead figures in the revision of the future leadership education. I did not sign up for the group, but I had several conversations with myself and my colleague Uma. I have a strong sense of responsibility for our leadership programme, and I have strong opinions about how the programme should be developed. At the same time, I still had too much work. Uma had earlier expressed her concerns over my workload and said that she thought it would be good for me to be a little invisible for a while. This comment struck me since I did not understand how invisibility could be a good thing, as I still felt a strong urge to be involved, gain influence, and be considered important for the process. However, I still had an overload of work, so I did not sign up for this group's work.

Grace came by and invited me to talk about organising the work around the development of our educational programme. Several colleagues had agreed to join the group, but she said that she wanted me to reconsider and join the group. She fanned the flames underlying my doubts about becoming a member of the group. Joining could also lead to more visibility towards the new colleagues. This context led to a conversation where I shared my experience of being invisible and felt a lack of recognition. She said that she did not share my experience of me being invisible at all and that I was one of few employees to whom she could leave any of our assignments. This comment was nice to hear, of course, but she had said that many times before, and it did not eliminate my feelings of dissatisfaction. At this moment, Grace had just had ten new employees from the merging University College, and I am sure that she was preoccupied with this.

We wrote all my tasks on the wall. After doing so, Grace pointed out that I had two overall responsibilities in the department and asked if it could be helpful to think about the different assignments from that perspective. I knew that she wanted me to join the group and work on developing the education, and I also knew that her agenda was to make me accept this assignment even though she knew that I had far too heavy a workload.  I felt that she was affirming me in order for me to accept this new task, while at the same time, I still felt there was room to refuse. My private conversations with myself were about the amount of work compared to the importance of the influence I would have by joining the group. Imagining not being part of the group made me feel almost claustrophobic and forced to participate. Looking back, I see that I was afraid of what decisions would be made about our programme, that I would have to adapt to afterwards. I wanted the influence, so I agreed to join, and another task landed on my plate.

## Initial reflections

This narrative is about how I refused to let Grace help me reduce the amount of work while at the same time continuingly experiencing too heavy a workload and a failure to thrive. I felt strongly about not wanting to betray anyone by backing out of the work assignments, and I wanted the influence that came along with participation. I felt invisible to the group of new colleagues, but I also realise that I did not feel recognised by Grace and Sally without knowing exactly why. Once again, my answer was to work on more activities and longer hours, still without feeling more visible.

I felt a threat to my sense of self if I could not be the person who was often needed and invited to help or contribute. I feared that if I withdrew, clients and colleagues would not invite me again. In hindsight, I also wanted the power that came with defining our leadership programme and who we were as an organisation. Gradually it became clear that wanting to be involved in almost everything might have made my influence less visible to myself and others and maybe even less significant in my own eyes. Acting like that has worked well for me over the years, so why did I suddenly respond, feeling invisible? I went from being the employee with significant organisational responsibilities to spending most of my time on smaller assignments, which seemingly nobody knew of, besides myself. The fact that I had more than enough work with the assignments that came to me from my client network, and not allocated from the management, had left me with an image of myself as not unique and significant anymore. This perception of myself seems to be a familiar companion and an ongoing part of my work/life processes.

In hindsight, I realise that I found myself in a conflictual situation since it is an important part of my identity to feel extraordinary and to stand out as a person. At the same time, I am not particularly eager to show off or to be too self-glorifying. Influenced by my upbringing, based on the *Law of Jante*, which I presented in my P1, I have learned not to be a show-off and that being extraordinary is only acceptable if you go the extra mile to help others. In a way, one could say that I have managed to be exceptional in the ways that are acceptable from the perspective of the *Law of Jante*, which in a sense can be seen as paradoxically special and not special at the same time. Linking this to my experience at the community meetings at the DMan, I see that my efforts to stand out as a person is about my work and not only about the way I feel about it. Being part of this community has brought me to see the importance of not separating the two. The implications might be that it is essential for me not to let people down and that my efforts might not be visible to others as I exert my influence more informally. I enhance my need for freedom and self-management which seems to make me anonymous to people who are not close to me. As a result of the merger, my lack of self-promotion towards the new managers and colleagues might have reinforced my invisibility experience. Success to me at the time was mostly about my contribution to the field we work within, which means helping or enabling leaders in the public welfare sector to do their best in their job, as opposed to gaining recognition from my management. I get frustrated when colleagues do not put their best efforts into their work because what we do is extremely important for the public sector and the managers. However, it was not in my relationship with our clients that I felt the failure to thrive, but rather with my co-workers and managers at the University College. This feeling of invisibility raises the question to whom and about what I want to become visible? When my learning set asked me this question, my answer was, "to our clients and students, the public managers that I try to help", but - based on the narrative - I tend to think that this answer needs to be more nuanced.

A group of my colleagues have the same degree of freedom in their jobs as I have, and I observe them being enrolled in the same pattern of having difficulties in saying *no* and rejecting assignments. My pattern seems to some extent to be recognisable to others in the organisation. We strongly value a large degree of self-management in our department, and I want to explore the concept of freedom in the way identities emerge in our work life and how I can take both myself and others into account in that process. Furthermore, I will inquire into my sense of self and my experience of visibility and invisibility in my everyday work life.

Based on my arguments in P2 about not losing the paradox of the individual and the social, I argue that responsibilities and how we stand out as successful are never individually held – they always imply several relationships. I will explore how this interdependence seems to entail inherent risks of losing the paradoxical understanding with the risk of losing my agency, being indecisive and feeling invisible. My animating question is: How can I understand the experience of invisibility, and what does this imply about freedom and identity?

## Sense of self and others

At the end of my P2, I was inspired by Mowles, who argues that *"a better-developed sense of self enables consultants paradoxically, a fuller exchange with the other"* (2009:292). In this project, my narrative is about not wanting to let down my co-workers, searching for influence, not being capable of reducing my workload and being left with a feeling of invisibility. However, I decided to ignore my manager's decision and, in a way, let her down. While in my P2, I focused on power and the disciplining of the self, this narrative raises questions about the degree of freedom and individual agency we experience in our relations to others.

One of the philosophers who referred to a dialectical approach to understanding the relationship between self and others was Hegel. In an attempt to re-actualise and interpret Hegel's *"Philosophy of Right"*, Axel Honneth states that the relationship between self and others in a Hegelian perspective is based on an understanding of "free" will. As quoted by Honneth, Hegel addresses the importance of *"the 'free' will having to will itself 'as free'"* (Honneth, 2000:26). Honneth elaborates, *"in order for the will to be able to will itself as free, it must limit itself to those of its 'needs, desires and drives'…"* (2000:26). While at the same time understanding autonomy as an unlimited *"experience of self"*, Honneth argues that Hegel presents a social understanding of freedom, in which entering into communication or participation in what he calls the epitome of just social order, is the way subjects can truly actualise their freedom (2000:27). Hegel describes free will in terms of "being with oneself in another" (2000:27) and compares it with friendship, where we are not only one-sidedly with ourselves but willingly limit ourselves in this process (2000:26). In this way, free experience of self is only possible when we know ourselves and voluntarily limit ourselves in recognition of others (2000:41).

As I understand this point, it addresses the paradoxical relation between freedom and limitation; subjects must limit themselves to recognise others' needs without sacrificing our own interests and identity to act. Freedom is understood as determinate indeterminacy or indeterminate determinacy, which underlines the paradoxical perspective of freedom and means that from this perspective, freedom is also inextricably linked to constraint. Losing this paradox might lead to losing the sense of oneself by not recognising one´s own wishes, or the sense of others, by not recognising them. This definition also underlines the interdependent relationship between the individual and the social, where *"freedom is to will something determinate, yet to be with oneself in this determinacy and to return once more to the universal"* (2000:26). A strong sense of self then comes along with our determinacy to limit ourselves on behalf of others. I would argue that determinacy and indeterminacy are part of a dialectical process of sensing oneself with others. In this understanding, the strong sense of self is not a phenomenon but an ongoing process in the relation between the individual and the social. In my narrative, I see that my strong wish to not disregard any of the people I work with makes me abandon my own needs.

The need for lesser work is overruled by my determination to be included and, therefore, not to let people down by rejecting invitations to help them. To some extent, it seems that I am unable to prioritise my tasks because I am lost in others' expectations towards me. At the same time, one might say that I am caught up with my own needs of being the employee who is always invited and perceived as being helpful and wanting the influence that might come along with participation.

Having a strong sense of myself as not wanting to let my co-workers down, and at the same time recognising my inability to do all this work to satisfactory quality, is simultaneously an expression of me being indeterminate and indecisive about who and what is more important to me. When holding on to the same response of fighting harder to perform and secure my significance to others, I held on to my identity as a helper, restraining me from thriving. In hindsight, I see that asking Grace for help expressed a necessity to deal with this push or pull on my identity. However, the way she wanted me to prioritise did not lead me to find a solution to do good in a Hegelian sense by actualising my free will as being with myself in another.

In my wish to meet all demands, I can say that I did not have the will or sense of self to be free and therefore left it up to Grace, while then insisting on my will to be free by not following her decision. This case illustrates the complex paradox determinacy-indeterminacy, as it reinforces that being free is not only about recognising our own interests and the interests of others. In this situation, I seem to think in a black or white manner about the choice – either I stop teaching and let down my colleague, or I let down my own need to have fewer assignments. However, acknowledging that we might need to abandon some of our own and others' interests while at the same time meeting other needs of both our own and others could have led me to further exploration of possibilities. Although I did do this subsequently with my teaching colleague, I see now that I lost the sense of my paradoxical freedom and constraint in this understanding since my experience of my own need to have less work seemed to be conflicting with my sense of ethical obligations to the people around me. This argument underlines the paradoxical relation between self and others and the contradictory elements in the continuing processes of becoming who we are. In this way, it is not a question of recognising our own interests or those of others as separate, but understanding our paradoxical interdependence and that this interdependence allows us to relate to ourselves, based on Hegel´s understanding of being with oneself in another (Honneth, 2000:41), even when it means that our world is based on contradictions. In my narrative, this perspective might not make the decision-making around my everyday work life easier. However, as Mowles states, Hegel's perspective offers an opportunity to *"admit the contradictions as they arise and then to pursue them systematically in thinking and discussing with others. …What is possible is greater insight, perhaps even greater comfort with some of the dilemmas that organising produces, but there is no suggestion of resolution or even of control"* (2015:34). Instead of relating to the contradictions, I see now that I discussed constraint with Grace and visibility and freedom with Sally. In my silent conversations with myself, I also did not manage to relate to the situation from this contradictive perspective.

Looking back now, I see that the insights from this narrative have made me practice the discipline of saying no to a greater extent than earlier. It has been difficult and anxiety-provoking for me to do this; I see that I miss out on influencing and belonging to some groups, but I also gain more time to do what I choose. Acknowledging the contradictions of the situation leads to a continuing negotiation of how to actualise freedom to recognise both myself and others. This context means a continuing negotiation about when to say yes or no and, in these processes, insisting on my free will as a social individual. As such, freedom is understood as a constant negotiation of when to say yes and when to say no in recognition of both myself and others and includes negotiation of self. In this way, the Hegelian perspective highlights the interaction or communication with both self and others in the processes of enacting freedom. He argues that through these processes of communication, we come to realise our freedom (Honneth, 2000:59), but how can I further understand the communication that leads to the situation of indecisiveness and my feeling of invisibility in the narrative?

## Communication between selves

If I was influenced by conventional literature on communication, I might think about sending and receiving a message from one person to another. Stacey and Mowles criticise this cybernetic perspective where individuals are regarded as autonomous actors, being separated or isolated from the world (2016: 83). In this regard, good communication is when *"translation processes are accurate and there is no 'noise' in the transmission"* (ibid). However, this perspective fails to include the interdependence between the individual and the social and instead understands the individual as being prior to the social (ibid).

To inquire further into the sense of self in processes of communication, I turn to the philosopher George Herbert Mead, who suggests an understanding that sees the relationship between self and other as paradoxical, and in which communication plays a central part. Hegelian ideas also inspired Mead. His work reflects an ongoing inquiry into the understanding of the self; he shares Hegel's understanding that selves only exist with other selves through communication (Mead, 1925: 278). As a result, Mead was preoccupied with forming selves and inherent processes of communication in the relationship between selves.

Mead understands communication in the broadest sense. He does not refer only to the spoken words but to tone, body language etc. He forms an understanding of communication based on a dialectical understanding of gestures and responses. He does not think of a sender or receiver but understands communication as one body gesturing to another, which leads to a response. The response can then be seen as another gesture back, which indicates a spiral perspective on communication as ongoing responsive processes (Stacey & Mowles, 2016:341). In Mead's view, it is through communication and the relation to others that meaning arises and selves develop by adopting the attitudes of others. Mead writes about the anticipation and perception of a group's attitudes, which he refers to as "the generalised other" (1934:154). In communication with ourselves and others, we anticipate the responses of others, which make us gesture with these anticipated responses taken into account. He indicates that people do not enter into communication processes as "empty" but come with a history of socially formed patterns of activity. Stacey and Mowles explain Mead's ideas: *"In order to accomplish complex social acts, it is not enough for those involved to be able to take the attitude of the small numbers of people they may be directly engaged with at a particular time. They need to be able to take the attitudes of all of those directly or indirectly engaged in the complex social act"* (2016:366). In people's practice of doing this, they cannot relate individually to everyone but take the attitudes of a few specific individuals and at the same time have the capacity to take the attitude of groups in a generalised form. Mead understands the generalised other as generalised attitudes or tendencies to act, evolving historically and always implicated in human interaction (Stacey & Mowles, 2016:366). In my narrative, this is illustrated in my communication by relating to my immediate co-workers and their anticipated response if I were to withdraw from my assignments. However, the idea of the generalised other indicates a more historically developed understanding of the anticipated response from others and leads to expectation towards my own response in the situation.

Through this process, I can see a pattern of losing my sense of self in the expectation that I would be judged self-absorbed and irresponsible in my relation to others. This anticipation of response might lead back to my childhood and how strongly the ideas of the *Law of Jante* have formed my way of interacting with others.

Mead elaborates on his perspective when he introduces the I-me dialectic in his understanding of self. Mead argues that selves are social in the process of taking the attitude of others in our view of ourselves (1925:284). He describes the I-me dialectic as *"The 'I' reacts to the self which arises through taking the attitudes of others. By taking those attitudes, we have introduced the 'me', and we react to it as an 'I'"* (Mead, 1934:174). In this way, he also indicates that selves emerge through communication, based on both external and internal processes of gesture and response and can also be seen as individuals' silent conversations with ourselves, which must be understood as radically social processes.

He states with his understanding of gesture-response that the response of others to a certain gesture tends to vary, based on the different life stories of the particular others. In this way, you can say that you do not know the meaning of your gesture until you experience the response from others, which might vary from one individual to another and from one situation to another. This temporal perspective and the related impact on communication indicate that the self is in a constant movement as the communication includes continuing gesturing-responding processes with new others. As such, the generalised other is also in a continuous movement. We continue to develop our perception of the generalised tendencies to act as we gain a new experience of responses. The self is in this way a social process between the gestures of the subjective "I" and the response from the "me", which are inseparable.

In my narrative, I realise that my relations with many others influence my conversation with Grace and my silent conversations about changing my situation about being too busy. I take the attitudes of selected specific others. However, with Mead's understanding, it seems central to reflect upon my actions from the perspective of my anticipation of the response of what he calls the generalised other.

As I understand Mead, he emphasises that my negotiations are not only with myself but simultaneously with my present clients, the colleagues involved in my tasks, my sons with whom I want to earmark a proper amount of time or my responsibility towards the DMan community. My negotiations are also about how I am historically intertwined with a specific way of relating to other people, and through this, I anticipate the responses I might receive. I see that my strong wish to help other people prevents me from saying no when people invite me into different tasks. My anticipation of the response is that they might not invite me again if I reject the invitation. Open invitations and the strong search for belonging to too many groups instead of belonging strongly to a specific group become central for my sense-making in the narrative situation. My need to keep as many doors open as possible to be understood as helpful and even invited to help, while at the same time having the possibility of escaping the disciplining that comes along with the membership of groups and the fear of exclusion or closed doors if I say no, leads me to feel significant and with difficulties in rejecting the invitations.

In Mead's understanding of self, the I-me dialectic is the foundation of human conduct. He introduces his understanding of intersubjectivity and the idea of human beings' "capacity of being several things at once" (1934:73). In my narrative, I see myself trying to be too many things at once. I wonder if the processes of becoming oneself might include the possibility of being several things in a state of indeterminate determinacy and losing the sense of this paradox and, with Honneth's perspective, getting lost in oneself or the other. I was getting lost in too many different expectations in my narrative with the result of me becoming indecisive.

I do not take a stand with what kind of employee I want to be to some extent. My strong wish to belong to many groups might mean that I have developed a capacity to be both teacher, consultant, researcher, salesperson and the team player, who is always there to support and help clients, colleagues and my manager. However, each of these roles could easily require a full-time job, so the capacity to be all of these must necessarily mean a choice of not doing any of them sufficiently. In my everyday organisational life with a high degree of self-management, I have not been aware of the consequences of wanting to be several things at once. Not being able to deselect any of my assignments is also a choice that comes with consequences. In our process of taking our experience seriously, my supervisor in the DMan community has commented several times that I seemed elusive and difficult to get to know. The idea of me being able to negotiate different sides of situated selves did not seem like a problem to me at the time, and her reflections did not make sense to me.

While working on this project, it has made me reflect on my pattern of belonging to many groups and its consequences. From the perspective of this narrative, I see now the importance of the processes through which we negotiate ourselves and risk losing the sense of either self or others. I see how I hold on to the pattern of belonging everywhere, which makes me lose a sense of myself to negotiate my way into belonging to many different groups. With this understanding, I believe that this introduces the paradox of being-becoming in a way where the processes of self are, at the same time, stable and unstable, predictable and unpredictable. In our interaction with ourselves and others, we bring in patterns of our historically embedded identity through communication based on our anticipation of particular others and the generalised other, indicating a personal history and identity we bring into new situations. However, the processes of forming the self are at the same time unpredictably changing as we enter into new relations and situations with other selves, also continuingly in the making. This process focuses on the ongoing negotiations of self and acknowledging that every choice comes with consequences and ongoing possibilities to choose differently.

Seemingly I faced two options in the narrative – to follow Grace´s decision or to keep working far too much. However, my negotiations with myself were far more complex and touched complex matters about my sense of self. When Grace tried to reduce the complexity, there seemed to arise a double bind of me being determined and indeterminate at the same time, as I insist on not taking a stand, which I see now was also the choice of a specific position. The sense of double-bind seems to emerge when I lose the paradoxical perspective and think that I can choose. My best solution in the situation was to find an alternative that again held on to my efforts to not turn my back on any of the people I worked with, including Grace, whose decision I did my best to avoid diplomatically. I held on to a pattern with the consequence of a continuing lack of thriving. Understanding individual and social as paradoxically interwoven does not seem to reduce the complexity and the difficulties I experienced in the narrative situations. To understand the special character of a paradox, Mowles is inspired by Hegel and states that,

> "There is no way to resolve the paradox and nowhere to stand outside of it; it generates itself and is ´self-grounding´: one concept calls out for its opposite, which is both defined and negated by it. Staying with the mutually negating ideas and noticing how it sends the mind moving, as uncomfortable as it may be, can provide further opportunities for reaching a more intense understanding of the paradox that one is experiencing" (Mowles, 2015:33).

Taking the paradox seriously and relating reflexively to the negating ideas, and even trying to gain more insight into the complexity of the emergence of ourselves might be the answer to complex paradoxical situations to find new ways of relating. However, in my narrative, not being reflexive about these patterns prevents me from discovering new ways of responding. Paradoxically, I get stuck in my old sense of self by maintaining a position from which I am included in as many groups or communities as possible. In this sense, I can see myself as elusively stable in my identity. However, I also experience in this narrative that one of the consequences of this way of interacting with myself and others at a certain point of time results in the experience of being invisible. Maybe I am stuck in a pattern where I tend to lose myself in the other because of a fear of being insignificant or invisible.

The reflections above and in my narrative relate to different potential reasons for my invisibility. However, I am puzzled by the understanding of invisibility as an undesirable feeling and how this can be related to the idea of freedom not being about freedom from constraints. I would like to inquire further into the understanding of visibility and invisibility as a radically social individual.


## Visible – invisible

Thinking about visibility and my experience of feeling invisible to others raises a question as to whom I want to become visible and why. The feeling of invisibility was entirely new to me and could have been evoked by several different elements as explored above. Visibility seems to require a more or less specified audience in order to see whatever we find visible. Looking back, I am embarrassed that I found myself trying to plan changes in my composition of assignments with Sally that would make this feeling of invisibility go away, believing that it was as simple as that. This experience brings me to an inquiry into invisibility and how to make sense of this.

In the last years before his death, the French philosopher Merleau-Ponty was interested in the visible and invisible character of human beings. The earlier and most well-known part of this work deals with a phenomenological perspective and a strong focus on the embodied practice of being in the world (Merleau-Ponty, 2014). Merleau-Ponty introduces an approach where visibility must be about the visible person´s relation to him/herself. Like Mead, Merleau-Ponty is interested in communication and responses. Merleau-Ponty introduces a focus on the flesh and addresses the communication of the bodily human. Some scholars argue that understanding the flesh is a relation between bodies, *"the connection between them that isolates each as a separate body and yet holds them all together in one world"* (Muller, 2017:221).

In contrast to a strong focus on language, Merleau-Ponty finds it essential to understand human communication as an embodied responsivity and not only from the perspective of a thinking inner subject (Thøgersen, 2015:235). In his latest working notes, published in "The Visible and the Invisible" (Merleau-Ponty, 1968), he argues for a new ontology. He introduces the metaphor of Chiasm, based on the Greek letter chi, which addresses his understanding of *"a dynamic diffraction or splitting dehiscence and mediating link between different sides of phenomena… For Merleau-Ponty, this opening chiasm is a processual patterning process of flesh that differentiates and 'unifies' without synthesis, while constituting all sensing, perceiving, and communication'"* (Helin et al., 2014:418-419). The idea that these opposites, thesis and antithesis, will lead to synthesis is, according to Merleau-Ponty, an idealisation. However, in my understanding, he emphasises that we have to accept and deal with complexity and ambiguity in our world.  *"The visible can thus fill me and occupy me only because I who see it, do not see it from the depth of nothingness, but from the midst of itself; I the seer am also visible"* (Merleau-Ponty, 1968:113). The chiasmic approach to human beings in the world leads to the understanding that people will always experience the world from a perspective, from where we become visible. When taking a specific perspective, this creates at the same time a blind spot, with the consequences of not discovering alternative understandings. Through this understanding, he signals that every moment of making sense of the world includes visibility and invisibility (Muller, 2017:185). The chiasmic approach means that two or more opposites of phenomena will be bodily experienced, including all the ambiguity. It brings to our attention that we are always visible as the participator in a situation, experiencing a phenomenon, in my case, a feeling of invisibility. In this way, my invisibility experience is somewhat different from Merleau-Ponty's perception of the phenomena. I become visible through the way I make sense of invisibility. My blind spot was that I did not recognise that being invisible in my organisation could also entail advantages. However, his perspective helped me to understand how I made sense of my embodied experience of invisibility and how I became visible as a self in the situation. Merleau-Ponty argues that experiencing the world in my way by idealising a feeling of visibility also creates an immanent degree of invisibility. The perspective from which this situation is experienced makes us visible while preventing us from experiencing otherwise. In my narrative, this is illustrated by my experience of invisibility as an unpleasant and unwanted feeling, making me blind towards Uma´s idea that it would be good for me to be a little invisible for a while. This situation indicates that I need to bring my attention to my own visibility as the person who experienced invisibility while at the same time acknowledging the invisibility and blindness towards other perceptions.

So, related to my feeling of being invisible, it would not make sense to focus on this theme without also addressing my own perception and visibility. Merleau-Ponty would argue that my own more or less conscious perception of invisibility must also be explored. Why do I consider the feeling of invisibility as something negative, combining it with – or even understanding it as – the main reason for my failure to thrive? When Uma suggests that I should be a bit more invisible, I see that it is a possibility, but I do not make sense of it as an attractive option. By perceiving the feeling of invisibility in this way, I am caught up in what Merleau-Ponty calls a bad dialectic approach. In contrast, he argues for what he calls a hyperdialectic. The hyperdialectic takes the understanding of chiasm seriously and does not restrict the plurality and ambiguity that comes along with this understanding. However, it resists the idea of recomposing being in a synthesis of the chiasmic opposites, which Merleau-Ponty calls the bad dialectic. He argues that;

> *"the good dialectic is that which is conscious of the fact that every thesis is an idealisation, that Being is not made up of idealisations or things said, as the old logic believed, but bound wholes where signification never is except in tendency, where the inertia of the content never permits the defining of one term as positive, another term as negative, and still less a third term as absolute suppression of the negative by itself"* (1968:94).

My interpretation of this is that he criticises dialectic perspectives that hold the illusion that if only thesis and antithesis are related, and maybe even articulated or reflected through embodied interaction, the novelty will arise, and new understandings emerge. My understanding is that he reinforces the contradictive and ambiguous nature of human life, from which we cannot escape.

This distinction between a good and a bad dialectic resonates with my narrative experience. Both my conversations with Grace and Sally and my silent conversations with myself do not envisage the plurality and the ambiguity in the situations. Through a short conversation about reducing my number of assignments or making sense and agreeing on reasons for my feeling invisible, we seem to believe that new possible solutions will arise and solve the problematic situation.

I see how we might again get caught up in the idea that we will create new desirable futures through dialogue. Especially in my last conversation with

Grace, we talked about our perceptions of being visible or invisible in the organisation. We tried to reach some synthesis instead of exploring the different perspectives of our disagreement and the complex nature of situations in organisations. We did not seem to find time to bring attention to contradictions and ambiguities without immediately eliminating these. Even though this could resonate with the social constructionist understanding of the world consisting of many truths, I find a significant difference. In my earlier work inspired by social constructionism, I found a strong focus on creating synthesis through language, which Merleau-Ponty's perspective problematises.

## Beyond relativism or dogmatism

Not considering anything as "the truth", but the world consisting as a multiverse of constructed truths (Gergen & Gergen, 2004) might lead to a position of relativism. Slife and Richardson argue that the social constructionist perspective leads to two choices – either dogmatism or relativism (2011:335). Regarding Gergen´s assumption that being free from dogmatism, people will do good things, they argue that his perspective is embedded in a dualism between tolerance and intolerance. This perspective relates to the intense focus on an appreciative approach, which is also a core perspective in the social constructionist ideas (Cooperrider & Srivastra, 1987). Social constructionists suggest that, if we talk positively about the future and focus on what we appreciate to do more of that, we can form positive futures through these dialogues (ibid), which I connect to Merleau-Ponty´s understanding of the bad dialectic.

The social constructionist perspective might lead to a lack of acknowledgement that people will not necessarily do good when liberated.

The unfettered faith in freedom might lead to relativism. "This relativism creates an absolute type of Enlightenment freedom that is ultimately a disorienting, meaningless freedom because it is more a *"freedom from" constraints and dogmatism than a "freedom to" do something important or good*" (Slife & Richardson, 2011:336). This perspective on freedom is far from the Hegelian perspective that emphasises the interconnectedness between freedom and constraint. Paying attention to this dualistic understanding within the social constructionist perspective, I see that I might have been caught up in failing to acknowledge some of the constraints in the narrative situation. I am not free to form my future work life with a more suitable workload through dialogue, and I do not feel visible again because Grace tells me that I am not invisible.

I agree with Slife and Richardson when they argue that everything is not up for grabs or for *"whatever co-actors prefer or choose to make of it"* (ibid:337). In the narrative, Grace and I fail to reflect on how we are both enabled and constrained in situations with no other goal than gaining insights from which we could move on together.

Merleau-Ponty's idea of hyperdialectic lends weight to the idea that my conversations with Grace were about whether it was true that I was invisible or not, maybe with the hope of creating some kind of synthesis that would make my feeling of invisibility go away. Even in accepting that we disagreed and even trying to explain our different perceptions, the conversation focused in an one-sided way on whether I was visible or invisible. I see now that reflection on what visible – invisible means to any one of us, and how we experience this in our everyday life in our organisation, might not make the difficulties disappear, but maybe we would become more aware of the complexity and both the freedom and limitation involved in the situation if we thought about it more directly.

What Merleau-Ponty adds seems to be the understanding that negotiations of identity are experienced bodily from the perspective of what he calls the seer, by which he also means the participant or observer. In this way, I find that he emphasises that the self, who is in the world and bodily experiencing this being, is always visible. Therefore, this visibility – that we do not experience the world from nothingness – is worth paying attention to. In my narrative, the perspective on invisibility was strongly perceived as negative in my understanding. In this way, I become visible in the situation and create blind spots that might have made sense with a different perception.

While Merleau-Ponty argues for a new subject-object understanding, Honneth and Margalit argue that perception must mean more than the concept of seeing (2001:113). Regarding the famous novel *The Invisible Man*, Honneth and Margalit relate invisibility to recognition (2001). They suggest that invisibility must be connected to the complex relationship of perception and expression that is played out between humans (2001:115). With this approach, they introduce the dimensions of both cognition and recognition. They argue that the *"act of recognition is due to an adding together of two elements: cognitive identification and expression"* (2001:116). First, the person is cognised as an individual in a specific situation, and secondly, the cognition results in some expression, which confirms the person's existence. This seemingly causal relation is, from my perspective, somewhat linear and slightly different to the dialectic approach as seen in Mead's understanding.  Bringing in Mead again, one could ask how processes of gesture-response lead to my experience of invisibility.

I see now that being invited to contribute is, in general, a gesture that makes me feel recognised and visible to others. When Grace tells me how much she values me as an employee, the positive affirmation is nice, but I do not long for it. In my conversation with Sally, we talked about how I generally felt side-lined when I heard about new larger assignments in our department in which I was not asked to play a part. The managers at the two levels above Grace were both new, and some of the initiatives they had taken were in areas where I had earlier been the key person. I see now that my identity and position as *the helper that gets invited* was threatened, which might have fanned the flame of the feeling of invisibility. The new management did not invite me, and I found that they invited some of my co-workers at times. In hindsight, I realise that my identity was partly made up of an idea of myself influencing things more indirectly without appearing to be a show-off. This trait made me invisible to the new managers.

I see that the consequence of not telling people much about what I have achieved is that it takes more time for others to learn about my expertise and invite me to contribute. After years of employment at the University College, I had become used to people knowing me, and suddenly, half of the staff did not, which I did not think of as a significant change in my work life at the time. This situation might have reinforced my experience of invisibility further and indicates how I have to become more aware of the temporal aspects of my interactions in everyday organisational life. Even though I had been part of the organisation for several years, it is never quite the same organisation, which is an argument for a continuing renegotiation of how we interact over time. I should have paid more attention to the need for renegotiation of my identity and my position in the organisation in a situation with new managers and co-workers.

Since my childhood, I have learned not to be a show-off. While at the same time wanting to feel important to others, going the extra mile in my wish to be extraordinary.  I see that I depended on others to recognise me by inviting me and confirming my significance, which comes with the dependence on others and the risk of getting lost in others. Making myself slightly more invisible for a while, as Uma suggested, would demand a larger degree of belief in myself because I would lower the participation that could eventually show me as an extraordinarily committed contributor in others' eyes. Getting lost in the other in this way also might mean developing a strong need for recognition from others. In an I-me dialectic perspective, one cannot separate the process of recognition into coming from oneself or others. However, we might be able to detach ourselves from our involvement with others in thought, providing the opportunity to reflect on these processes of being oneself with others.

A strong sense of self in this perspective is not something you can achieve once and for all or without others. A strong sense of self is an ongoing process with others. We continuingly reflect on our own identity in the way it emerges paradoxically and in ambiguity, with the effort to escape from simplified idealisations.


## Reflection and reflexivity

It seems to be a commonly expressed idea that the answer to meet the challenges of modern work life is to develop one´s capacity to reflect on the way we want to be and become individuals or to become reflexive. Even though reflection and reflexivity have often been used synonymously, several scholars have argued for a significant difference between the two (Cunliffe & Jun 2005, Hibbert, 2012 & Mowles, 2011). Where the perspective on reflection is based on a tradition of mirroring the way we think (Schön, 1983), reflexivity is thought of as one's ability to think about the way we have come to think, acknowledging that one can never become a neutral observer (Stacey & Mowles, 2016:35-36).

Understanding the strong sense of self as an ongoing process is presented by Mead as a reflexive process and indicates the need for reflection and reflexivity.

> *"You have seen that the term 'self' is a reflexive affair. It involves an attitude of separation of the self from itself. Both the subject and the object are involved in the self in order that it may exist. The self must be identified, in some sense, with the not-self. It must be able to come back at itself from the outside. The process, a process within which both of the phases of experienced life, a process in which these different phases can be identified with each other - not necessarily as the same phase but at least as expressions of the same process"* (Mead, 1936:88).

Even though most scholars emphasising reflection or reflexivity agree that it is impossible to take the role of an independent observer, the most pervasive perspective on reflexivity still seems to indicate to some extent that we can take a detached perspective on ourselves. Mead and Merleau-Ponty offer two supplementing perspectives, which shed light on how we can understand the involved detached position of reflection or reflexivity.

As explained above, Mead advocates in his understanding of the I-me dialectic how we as radically social selves always emerge through social processes with others. Gaining detachment through reflexivity means constant paying attention to our interdependence on others, both present and as the generalised other. His focus is, however, mainly on the mind even though he does acknowledge embodiment, while Merleau-Ponty encourages us to take ourselves as an object to ourselves but argues that *"reflection recuperates everything except itself as an effort of recuperation, it clarifies everything except its own role*" (1968:33). With his chiasmic approach (Low, 2000:33-34) and the perspective on the subject as a body, Merleau-Ponty introduces a hyperreflection, in which he brings attention to the way we are always in our body of experience and unable, therefore, to explain a phenomenon or a situation as an observer that is not bodily involved.

Reflexivity or hyperreflection involves the awareness of our being in the world, with its various histories and traditions embedded. Even though he argues, in his perspective on visible – invisible, that we will always have blind spots in the way we relate to the world, he does not seem to determine to what extent one is still strongly biased when relating reflexively to oneself. Mowles distinguishes between reflection and reflexivity as two separate, yet connected, activities: *"In reflecting we will be thinking and feeling deeply about something, possibly our own experience, whilst in becoming reflexive we are bringing that reflection back to ourselves and may be changed by it"* (2015:60).

As I understand Merleau-Ponty, his idea of hyperreflection also addresses that we can reflect on what is going on for us, but we also need to think about how we think about it. In this way, both Merleau-Ponty and Mead emphasise the idea of taking ourselves as an object and combining the two makes us understand self-reflexive processes as involving both body and mind.

Merleau-Ponty´s chiasmic understanding pays attention to a tendency to idealise the one side of the chiasm, as I do in my narrative through the idealisation of visibility. The chiasmic approach addresses the two sides of an aspect. However, when taking the perspective of paradox, *"two mutually exclusive self-referencing ideas define each other, but negate each other at the same time"* (Mowles: 2015a p.3).

I argue for a reflexive approach that takes account of the paradoxes in the organisational life, in this narrative towards visible-invisible, where we can discover our idealisations and move into a paradoxical approach to organisational life with the immanent ambiguities we experience. Having said this, I understand the different perspectives on both reflection and reflexivity as being strongly combined with thinking. To take Merleau-Ponty´s perspective on the body seriously, I find it important when Mowles stresses that reflexivity is about bringing both thoughts and feelings back to ourselves. In this understanding, reflexivity should be both a cognitive and an embodied practice – the latter seemingly insufficiently illuminated in organisational studies.

Understanding the self as a reflexive affair, I have come to see the substantial amount of freedom in my job, which I have found of great value in order to be able to create my own job and self-manage to a large extent. I see now that the idealisation of this freedom has prevented me from paying attention to the negative consequences of this idealised understanding of freedom as being without constraints. My way of responding to freedom has been an individualised effort to try to live up to all the expectations, maintaining the position as the helper and the person who carried a huge workload in order to belong to as many groups as possible, but who did not step forward to show my impact or influence. When I failed to succeed with that, I blamed myself because these were my choices, and my answer was asking for help, only to be able to continue on my own again.

By losing my understanding of the paradox between individual and social, I have found myself distancing myself from belonging too strongly, which has provided me with a false sense of freedom and fragmentation from a shared responsibility with my colleagues around me. Not paying attention to these patterns of gesturing-responding, I see now that the missing acknowledgement of both the positive and negative outcome of my way of interacting with others with a sense of freedom had the consequence of me not feeling visible to myself or others.

## Summing up

In this project, I have come to think that developing a strong sense of self must address the interrelation and the paradoxical relation between self and others. The negotiation processes of selves include our historically and culturally formed identity in the making of our present selves. These processes of self are played out through interaction in the broadest sense of a dialectic gesturing and responding. This process entails paying attention to the language and the way our bodies interact, which emerge in the present based on both history, cultural influence, and our anticipation of the future.

I have found that being a member of, or relating to, multiple groups in organisations include the risk of experiencing indeterminacy and invisibility. My urge to create or maintain membership or invitations to join different groups has the consequence of me "getting lost in the other". The anticipated response from others to my saying no to assignments included a risk of exclusion or not being invited again.

Being preoccupied with too many tasks and expectations from others led to a feeling of invisibility, even though seemingly one should think that staying out of assignments was the more obvious way to invisibility. In this way, freedom is neither to abstain from belonging to groups with the disciplining that comes with this membership, nor is it necessary to not engage in many assignments. However, freedom must include processes of negotiating identity where we understand ourselves as being both enabled and constrained at the same time, but with consideration of both our own needs and the needs of others, without neglecting attention to any of these dimensions.

My decision to not take a managerial position and not have a more formal power position at the University College, and at the same time no longer being responsible for a larger assignment attracting organisational attention, might also have had consequences. Parallel to this, the merger included new members of our organisation who did not know me or had any visible formal signs of my expertise. My pattern of depending on invitations to help others made me feel a lack of recognition, and my understanding of my bodily reaction was that of me being invisible. I did not see the merger as having a strong impact on my way of working. In hindsight, I see that this might have reinforced my experience of being invisible.

The feeling of invisibility might have emerged for several reasons, as suggested in this project. The idealisation of being visible was characteristic of my way of making sense of the world. The paradox of visible - invisible is another element worth taking seriously. Through reflexivity, we might be aware of how we tend to idealise. The fact that we are always visible in how we interact and make sense of the world is combined with immanent invisibility, a perspective not taken, and through this, following blind spots. The importance of a reflexive approach to both of these and to the ambiguities and contradictions we experience in everyday organisational life is reinforced in this project. Further, the idea of creating ideal organisational realities through dialogue and synthesis is argued to be impossible and that we must be careful not to fall into idealisations in an attempt to avoid the ambiguous and paradoxical character of organisational life.

Freedom and enhanced individual agency might or might not emerge from exploring interdependencies, contradictions, ambiguities and possible idealisations. The reflexive way of relating to these organisational life elements must be based on both cognitive and embodied processes of taking oneself as an object. In this reflexive position, every individual will always be biased in the perspective on oneself since one can never take a detached position in a fixed way. To continually develop the capacity to be reflexive, we must join in collaborative reflexivity with others.

Getting lost in others or oneself seems to have the consequence of people being fragmented. Losing the sense of the paradox of individual and social experience might result in a lack of cohesion in the way we work and understand ourselves.

My new understanding of freedom gives rise to an attention towards the possibility of evolving new communities in modern organisational life. Freedom might emerge from belonging to groups in recognition that we are both enabled and constrained and when we simultaneously take our own needs and the needs of others into account. In this, a strong sense of belonging to a group will not mean lesser individual freedom or agency. However, we might all experience continuing contradictions that lead to the negotiation of our identities.

In my further research, I want to inquire into how people can continue to become visible to themselves and others and build strong communities around reflexive practice in order to be able to do their jobs. Inspired by Dewey, I want to explore the idea of freedom further: *"for we need freedom in and among actual events, not apart from them"* (Dewey, 1922:199). I am also inspired by Dewey´s ideas on democracy concerning the development of sustainable organisational cohesion.

# Project 4 – Standing firm with fragile feet on volatile ground

## Introduction

My understanding of my role in facilitating leadership development has changed during the course of my research on the DMan programme. I find myself increasingly critical of leadership programmes aiming to control managerial behaviour by claiming to be able to create a highly specific and predictable output in leadership competencies and even actions in the organisation. Instead, I find that encouraging reflexivity to make sense of what people are already doing together in organisations is an alternative and meaningful way of facilitating leadership development. From this perspective, processes of leadership development do not imply an absence of intentions or goals but highlight the unpredictable nature of the emergence of organisational behaviour.

With insights from my earlier projects, I have paid attention to the fact that ambiguity, contradictions, conflicting situations, and paradoxes are inevitable parts of organisational life.  It is necessary for leaders to accept and relate to that reality. I also argue that members of organisations tend to try to avoid the ambiguity by idealising one perspective over another instead of thinking that contradictory elements can be parts of the same processes. Such idealised understandings come with the risk of being lost in oneself and being unable to see the perspective or need of others or being lost in another and forgetting to hold on to your own sense of self. When we reduce the complexity and acknowledge the contradictory elements of life, this process might lead to indeterminacy, as suggested in my project 3

(Honneth, 2000). By acting as indeterminate, we seem to think that one can suppress or avoid conflict as a consequence of difference and contradictions and might end up with an invisible sense of self. This experience has been mine, and, as I will go on to explain in this project, it seems to be relevant to others too.

In my practice, this process means paying attention to my pattern of wanting to belong to many groups and, therefore, ending up with an experience of invisibility or an elusive sense of self.  My effort of being myself *with* others, and through this finding ground for working within processes of leadership development, is the situation where the following narrative unfolds. In my job, I engage in different tasks with different kinds of clients, students or co-workers all the time, when I am assigned to consultancy jobs, teaching commitments, coaching, internal development work, etc. The narrative for this project is about a current consultancy job and the beginning of this process will be presented in the following narrative.


Narrative – surprised by change in relationships
In August 2019, a new set of governmental rules in the field of youth and education came into effect. One of the elements in the new law is that all Danish municipalities are obliged to coordinate the different sector-specific efforts they make in order to help young citizens to get educated or employment.  I was intrigued when the project manager, Molly, from a Danish municipality called with a request for me to contribute to an internal process for implementing the new rules. She explained their ambitions about wanting all managers to share the responsibility for this effort. They wanted me to help kickstart the development of a collaborative community

between the group of managers, and it would only take one day of my time to come and tell them about what they, from my perspective, would have to deal with. I admired their courage in not placing responsibility with one manager, since that, in my experience, is what most organisations do, so I agreed to make a one-day programme for ten managers.

My presentation in the one-day seminar addressed my understanding of collaboration and how it is, to some extent, an idealisation of how to solve problems in the organisation and that collaborative practice in my perspective would also present them with new challenges. I told them about power struggles they should expect and how they would meet differences and contradictory interests and face interpersonal conflicts. I asked them whether they had a culture of disagreement or a culture of dishonesty and what culture they might want to encourage in the future. It felt right to be a bit provocative since I found that collaboration across contexts had been proposed as the future answer to many of the challenges in the Danish welfare sector. I felt obliged to challenge this idealisation, and as a consultant believed that I had to disrupt or nuance their understandings. I had the feeling that I was walking a thin line between helping them to move on and simply leaving them with their problems, since I did not present them with any solutions to their challenges but instead claimed that working closely together would just give rise to other conflicts and problems. I was aware that this kind of consultant behaviour could entail the risk of them not thinking of me as helpful because I did not teach them how to create shared responsibility. However, I felt the freedom of not having to be a salesperson or responsible for specific results but focusing on explaining my own beliefs and inviting them to think about the implications, without having to make sure they liked me afterwards.

Despite my own sense of having disturbed their understanding of the idealisations of collaboration, they responded with openness and engaged in reflections with curiosity.  Looking back, I understand that I had faced what I perceived as a risk when I did not adopt the idea of collaboration as the answer to all problems regarding young citizens, nor did I act as the hero who knew what they should do. However, the idea of focusing on collaboration, and the way we work together in organisations, is a very important theme for me, which, in hindsight, might have been obvious to the participants in my engagement. My presentation resonated with the participants and helped them realise that they needed to view collaboration as an ongoing process of negotiation between each other with the result that they no longer talked about the wish for change as an implementation project that would end.

After this event, I was asked to run a similar one-day seminar for an extended group of managers in the same organisation, which resulted in more reflective dialogues. Later the project manager requested a presentation about how we could move on together in a shared process over the next year.  I was very motivated and full of energy because it made sense to me to be able to work with leadership development in this way where we had moved away from talking about project implementation and wanted to pay attention to an ongoing process of working closer together around the joint task with young citizens.

I described an ongoing process where the group of managers were to critically reflect on their experiences as a group working to share responsibility for education or jobs for more young citizens. I presented a programme, with no predefined themes, but where we would choose a theme for every gathering together, based on the emerging experiences and challenges, and on the aspiration to become a reflexive and collaborative management team. The group of managers that planned to join consisted of the same participants who attended the two first one-day seminars and eight new managers (from here on referred to as the large group). In the negotiations with the project manager and four managers (the planning group), we agreed that the large group should meet for one half a day every six weeks for the subsequent year.

## The first meeting in the large group

I was full of excitement and anticipation when I entered the doors of the municipal building, and the project manager showed me to our room. I was certain that this way of working with managers would seem helpful and would provide them with a sense of meaning and agency in their shared efforts. Based on my former experiences with a number of the participants, I obviously expected to be engaged in more explorative conversations and reflections. However, time would show that I was about to be surprised.

We entered the district council meeting room with paintings of the former mayors on the wall. There was an atmosphere of seriousness in this room, and a sense of formality emanating from the microphones in each place, reinforcing my sense of anticipation, as if a seminal process was about to start. The last couple of weeks, I had been thinking about the contradictory feelings that had only recently occurred for me regarding this assignment. On the one side, I was happy to have the possibility to work with the group in this way.  This feeling was based on my best judgement for what would be helpful for the managers. On the other hand, it felt like a huge burden of responsibility resting on my shoulders. What if we failed to succeed? What if all this reflection would lead to absolutely no change? Furthermore, even worse, what if the efforts did not help the socially vulnerable young citizens? I felt my whole identity as a professional was at stake here.

Happy, friendly faces entered the room. As they were walking in, I heard what I perceived as extremely joyful conversations, and the room was filled with laughter which also brought a smile to my face.  At the same time, I was wondering whether that amount of laughter was covering over some issue. My attention towards idealisations made me wonder whether participating in this programme could be all joyful and positive, or what kind of political game was going on here. My legs could not stand still, and I kept walking restlessly around the room. I felt observed and did not know what to do with myself. I just wanted to get started, maybe as an attempt to escape from the tension I felt.

Since even more managers were included in the group, we started by presenting ourselves after the planning group of managers introduced the organisational ambitions and how this process had evolved. In my introduction about working as a large group, I presented my ideas of reflecting together as a way of dealing with the unpredictability involved in the work they were engaging in together. Then, I asked them to go into smaller groups and begin to negotiate what would be essential for them in our creation of a learning space. In the middle of this exercise, I particularly noticed a couple of comments addressed to me personally from one of the new participants about how they could not read the slides from the managers´ presentation. A feeling of unfairness arose in me as she implied that this was my responsibility, even though it was part of the managers' presentation. However, I responded with a friendly smile and nodded to show that I recognised the input since I did not want to be critical or provocative just yet.

When working in the smaller groups, some groups went behind closed doors, while others stayed in the room or found corners outside in the hall. In general, I felt both excited and a bit awkward in my own role, which made me care about how I stopped by to listen. A feeling of constraint emerged from being more concerned about what they might think of me, rather than participating in the dialogues with my own ideas in relation to what they were talking about. There seemed to be a wall between the participants and me, indicating how I was both invited into this group and at the same time an outsider.  Compared to my earlier engagements in this process, where I had felt more relaxed and included, this perception was suddenly an unexpected experience that made me hesitant about my relationship with the participants. I tiptoed my way into the groups, just listening to their conversations, almost apologising with my facial expression if they noticed my presence. My inability to negotiate my participation with the small groups at that stage made me distance myself from them.

There seemed to be a lot to share in the group conversations – they were talking a lot and seemed to be very engaged and animated. However, I thought to myself that their conversations were very focused on the actions of others, so I asked myself how one enables a process of reflexivity and taking oneself as an object of attention?  How would I know if we were going in the right direction?

As if surrounded by tigers who were prepared to attack, the only conversation I had with the small groups was when some groups briefly asked me about the time or whether I thought they were doing the task right. My chest tightened. I felt trapped and only wanted to escape from this old-fashioned way of understanding the role of the consultant, being in control of the process. In the plenary presentation that followed, one group highlighted the importance of getting to know one another in the large group. This comment made me relax my breathing since I took this point to mean that several of the other participants shared my understanding of all of us being responsible for what emerged in the room.

Later, when we had a break for coffee, Molly came to me pointing to the fact that people were talking to each other across typical organisational structures and with others with whom they did not usually interact. Another manager who had been part of the planning group from the beginning also addressed me and told me that he would rather that the ones present were engaged and motivated than demanding for everyone to stay part of the group process.

Looking back, I am not sure if they were both trying to calm themselves or me down, by pointing to positive things or addressing how it would be acceptable if some of the participants did not want to continue in these processes. My answer was that hopefully lack of motivation for the shared task, both at these meetings and in their wider collaboration, was also something we would be able to address in the large group. He nodded; however, I felt uncertain about how he made sense of what I was saying. With hindsight, I wonder if he said this because there was an expectation for everyone to be happy about being part of this group and maybe that led to the extreme positivity or whether he sensed my tension about how to relate and wanted to make me more relaxed. I was wondering whether we were about to form a group in which there was only room for motivated participants, and I felt it was wrong to exclude the more concerned or even resistant voices.

Maybe as a result of the power relations in the room, the presence of different management levels, or the fact that some managers had been part of this group for much longer than others, the focus on production and action was reinforced in the conversations. It became clear to me that the reflexivity I had experienced on the first two seminars was not repeated on this day. When we ended the day by talking about possible themes for our next gathering, some of the managers seemed to be competing over having more answers about how to be able to collaborate. I felt that the process was like a balloon without gas. I was disappointed with the results of the day, and even though I wanted to take their ideas seriously and wrote them all down thoroughly, I did not find most of the suggestions particularly helpful for them. I found myself wanting to place them all in a large circle as a way to enable the kind of conversation I found helpful while thinking it would be too disturbing for them, but I felt strongly drawn to help them get a reflexive perspective on what they were doing. I reminded myself that for this group, it was only their first meeting and that I should pay attention to my own ambitions and have more patience with the process.

Looking back, I made a judgement about how this group was not ready to share their vulnerabilities openly with each other very early on that day, which draws my attention to the fact that I am also part of the process of this sense of readiness. Might they have been ready if I had challenged them more and did my hesitancy to challenge them result in the lack of reflexivity?

My ambition was for them to take themselves as objects to themselves in order to be able to reflect on their own part of what went on in this group, maybe even reflexively exploring the underlying assumptions of their way of interacting as managers. I was convinced that this practice might help them to gain detachment from their involvement with each other in order to become aware of the patterns of behaviour they wanted or needed to change. Instead, I heard them talking about how they would suggest an information system that would secure collaboration. In my eyes, they were looking for answers outside of themselves, as if the change had nothing to do with their own motives and understandings, which frustrated me since I did not believe in such answers and worried that we would not be able to go on together. I was afraid that turning it into the very concrete problem-solving process would prevent us from reflecting on how the managers experienced their collaboration in their everyday work.

## Initial reflections after the first meeting

The dilemmas in this narrative are symptomatic of the crisis in my work that arise when I am trying to work out what to achieve as a facilitator. I was first invited into this municipality six months before the first meeting in the large group with the task of helping managers move on in a new, more collaborative way. I see that doing so has already made me interact very differently compared to my first meetings with managers in this assignment. However, what I find myself doing might be seen as an attempt to disrupt what has become the well-known practice of consultants for both myself and the participants and our shared assumptions behind it.

Reading Merleau-Ponty led me in my P3 to suggest that we tend to idealise one side of a chiasmic life.  As mentioned in the narrative, my ambition is for managers to gain detachment from their involvement (Elias, 2001:104 & Mowles, 2015:51-52) in their everyday work life, to discover their part in the power relations, their own perspectives, understandings or idealisations; a process through which new interactions, new identities and new involvement might or might not emerge.  I question their understandings, while at the same time trying to sense the anxiety and sensitivity that comes along with this process. My constant question to myself is about how to find the appropriate amount of disturbance even though I do realise that this is not "something" I can find. However, in this narrative, I started questioning my own ambitions about change. Is it also just another idealisation when I encourage reflexivity from other people, but got almost annoyed when they seem to repeat their interactions, and not change? Is my critical approach preventing me from appreciating the small things, like acknowledging how the managers start talking to others in new constellations and the consequences that might come along with this? I see how I am caught up in an eagerness to change organisational life, and that I find it hard to accept if others might not understand the disruption of their perspectives as meaningful or easy.

In recognition of my arguments from the previous projects, the power relations I am part of and the freedom to become a professional based on a strong sense of self as well as being oneself with another, does not help me with discovering a firm understanding of what I do. My best account for my work would be that I invite managers into an interaction that might lead to new insights and through this to creating new everyday management practices to benefit the Danish welfare sector. This process emphasises the interdependence with the people I work with and my vulnerability caused by the pressure to succeed as a consultant if success equals change in behaviour and practice. Looking back on the first meeting with the large group of managers raises the question as to how I can make sense of what I do, when what I do is so dependent on others, with whom I am just a temporary leader and one out of many participants? With this uncertainty, I moved on with my work in the Danish municipality.


## The meeting in the planning group

After the first meeting in the large group, I met the planning group, who were four of the managers who initiated a plan for more collaboration more than a year earlier, and Molly. They represented different units of the organisation and had all been working closely together, sharing the ambition of closer collaboration – even before the new law was issued.

Based on my disappointment with the results of the day, I felt both anxious and determined going to the meeting. I decided that I wanted to exemplify in the meeting how conversations about complex matters and decision-making might be, so I wanted to participate in a way that invited them to reflect with me. I was certain that I would not accept an invitation to be the heroic consultant, who knew what to do next, so I chose to share my doubts based on my observations at the first meeting. A feeling of remaining indeterminate in a determinate way, and the awareness of danger in not appearing as a competent consultant, followed me to the door of the meeting room.

I was joining the planning group that late afternoon. It felt familiar. The cosy office was immediately welcoming with coffee, candy and grapes. The room felt relaxed and suffused with a sense of well-being, which immediately made me feel included. As we opened the meeting, I told them that I would be curious as to hear their reflections based on the first meeting, before I would tell them how I was making sense of my observations and that this might lead to ideas for the next meeting in the large group. They caught me by surprise since they did not respond with a focus on concrete actions as I had anticipated. The tension and the focus on information systems and actions as experienced in the large group were insignificant in the conversation that emerged. After opening the meeting by inviting to them to articulate their reflections, my self-consciousness and determination in not taking the role of the heroic consultant seemed unnecessary, and we just joined in mutual reflections based on each other's input.

We shared observations about the positive engagement and decided that we should trust the expressed interest in the programme and appreciate how people joined conversations in new constellations. We explored our experience of one group of managers holding on to a stronger sense of autonomy than the others and how come they might do so. We questioned our own parts and whether we could disturb what we all recognised as a general pattern. How could we find ways of inviting them into the group?

When we talked about whether to raise this with the whole group of managers, one of the planning group members – Albert, the manager of a drop-in centre – expressed his reservations. He was worried that he would be seen as critical and negative. I reflected that similar worries might be silencing some of the other managers in the larger group. A feeling of concern arose as we continued. At the meeting in the large group, I had asked for inputs for the next meeting, and through our conversation at this meeting, we approached the decision that their wish for knowledge through an information system was not the right way to go in our next meeting. I shared my concern that we did not listen, and we agreed that the need for information should still be addressed as a need to get to know more about each other. Albert said that he thought they needed more time for these conversations and suggested speed dating and more time to talk together in general.  This moment took me by surprise. I rarely experience managers who want to spend more time, sharing conversations between colleagues to get to know one another. However, I felt relieved once again, as if my thoughts about leadership development could unfold within this group.

Time was running out, and some of the managers had to leave. I felt a pressure to conclude, so I tried to think out loud. I summarised what I took with me from the conversation and that I would try to create a process that would address some of the difficult themes, but also sharing with the large group how we were taking the input from their group seriously by doing this. On my way back, I felt relieved by the response to my concerns, and I felt that the (time) pressure to move in the right direction was no longer as hard.  I had a sense of belonging to this group, while still being an outsider, but did not feel awkward. The interaction in this group felt familiar and I found it easy to participate. I felt my role as a consultant was still being negotiated and that the process of being myself *with* others would be an ongoing task. At the same time, I felt caught up in a feeling of standing strong and fragile at the same time. My interdependence to negotiate my role left me with the agency to participate and yet a sense of freedom with this group. At the same time, I knew that I could not be certain that this experience would last.


## Further reflections

At this subsequent review meeting, I was surprised by Albert's request for more time for conversations. My experience is that I often have to negotiate the importance of spending time on the conversation before we move on because managers in my experience are often in a hurry.  In a way, I was happy to hear this comment, which relieved me from a tightening burden. However, it brings me back to the question of pace. My ambitions, as they emerge in the narrative, can also be connected to time and how we might expect change from one another. Had I rushed the processes and if so, what had made me act differently compared to the earlier meetings in this municipality?

The atmosphere at the meeting makes me wonder how settings and interactions change from time to time. Why was it that in the first two seminars before the large group meeting, we engaged in reflection based on rather provocative statements? Why could disagreements and doubts be expressed easily in the planning group without much tension? In the planning group, we were able to talk about how patterns of collaboration seemed different in different sectors, and we even spoke openly about concerns to voice these reflections in the large group.

In my inquiring into the topic of freedom and the movements of identity, my reflections led me to think about how identities are at work in leadership development processes.  It made me realise how we tend to idealise individual freedom when we expect managers to be able to change their behaviour and their way of interaction just because they are told to or if they find it meaningful. My own struggle and determination to stay indeterminate as a consultant showed how difficult it is to hold on to your sense of self when historical and powerful understandings of the competent consultant invite you to take a specific position. This experience makes me reflect on what kind of similar struggles the managers face. The ongoing negotiations of identity do not come with an individual choice to be the manager you chose but constitute a social process. I want to explore how participants in leadership development processes like this might experience a threat to their identity and more or less agency in order to change their identity as a leader. The animating question for this project is: What are the consequences of the ongoing demand for change in identity in leadership development processes?

## Rhythms of change

I argued in my project 2 that the emerging character of organisational life cannot be managed or controlled completely. Therefore, it also cannot be understood as a result of rationally planned nor controlled processes. This conclusion draws me away from a more conventional understanding of organisational change as linear processes involving predetermined steps as presented by, e.g. Kotter (1995), and refers to the emergent character of organisational life as described in my P2.

My experience of entering into different and changing spaces of interaction in the different groups in this narrative, and the ambitious demands for pace in the wish for change in managerial behaviour, makes the work of Henri Lefebvre relevant. Through a dialectical approach to time and space, he introduces what he calls rhythmanalysis to convey an argument about the importance of paying attention to rhythms of everyday life (2019). Although his work concerns everyday life and not more specifically working practices, I find that his focus on entanglements between mind, body, time and space and the repeating and changing ways in which people engage is very relevant to understanding the changing character of our interactions in the narrative.

Lefebvre was a Marxist philosopher and sociologist born in 1901. He had the ambition to turn the concept of rhythms into a new science, with the attempt of getting us to think about space and time differently by linking them together from a dialectical perspective (2019:3). His impression was that Marxists over-emphasised the temporal dimension of everyday life while sacrificing the spatial, and this dialectical perspective resonates with my critical approach to idealisations of one side of a chiasm over another, as argued in my P3. This approach also means that his idea of rhythm is not to be confused with movement, and he argues that *"we tend to attribute to*

*rhythms a mechanical overtone, brushing aside the organic aspect of
rhythmed movements"* (2019:16). He pays attention to repetition as a
central element of his understanding of rhythm. He wants to put a lid on the
idea that repetition excludes difference but argues that repetitions give
birth to difference (2019:17). My understanding of this is that he addresses
the contradictory elements not only as coexisting opposites but as mutual
prerequisites for each other. In general, he argues that understanding
rhythm analysis must be based on the unfolding of several moving
oppositions and *"...does not isolate an, object, or a subject, or a relation. It
seeks to grasp a moving but determinate complexity"* (2019:21). This
perspective on the subject, object and relationship also corresponds with
the dialectic perspectives of both Mead and Merleau-Ponty where individual
and social interactions can only be understood as paradoxically interrelated.

Lefebvre introduces the idea of polyrhythmia, which also brings focus to the
body; thus, he argues that *"the rhythmanalyst calls on all his senses. He
draws on his breathing, the circulation of the blood, the beatings of his heart
and the delivery of his speech as landmarks"* (2019:31). This analysis also
means that he argues that a rhythmanalyst *"will not be obliged to jump from
the inside to the outside of observed bodies; he should come to listen to
them as a whole and unify them by taking his own rhythms as a reference by
integrating the outside with the inside"* (2019:30). In my understanding, this
approach means paying attention to what is going on in the situation by
listening both to myself as a consultant and to others in order to understand
the ongoing rhythms of time and space.

The awkwardness in negotiating my role in the smaller group conversations
seemed like a change in rhythm compared to my earlier ways of relating to
some of these managers. When I approached some of the groups, my body
became tense and I found it difficult to join the conversations. Suddenly I

was caught up in thinking about how they would think of me if I interfered too much with their conversation and I did not think of myself as a natural part of their dialogues. Earlier on, in the one-day seminars, I had felt included as an equal participant in the process of exploring new ways of moving on together.

Thinking back on my first one-day introduction seminar with these managers reminds me of a tennis match. As I wrote in my narrative, my presentations could have been perceived as provocative, not presenting the conventional solutions expected from a consultant.  By not presenting solutions and without any specified expectations of a change in their practice, one could argue that I might have changed the rhythm of the leadership seminar. No matter what kind of difficult ball I threw at them and how big a risk I felt came along with it, they responded with interest, curiosity and invited me to play along with them in their movement of thought.

Gathering in the larger group for our first meeting, the smoothness of the interaction did not seem to exist in the same way. The atmosphere was different even before the participants entered the room; there was another sense of seriousness in the room, and I was already worried that I could not live up to the expectations of reflexivity leading to the change they wanted. I felt intimidated by the anticipation of hearing them think that I was not as good as they had expected. By paying attention to my clumsy efforts to join the work in the smaller groups, and how I felt alienated in my interactions and afraid to be left alone with the responsibility, brings me to think about others and their possible difficulties in negotiating their way into the group. Maybe they also experienced tension in their way of relating to other managers and even other managers of managers. Perhaps the group had become increasingly full of different individuals trying to find their way to relate to various others in this specific setting. It does not answer my question about whether more or less time to get to know each other or negotiate their ways into the new large group would have been helpful.

However, my own difficulties and tensions in relating to the other participants make me think about the larger group and how some of us had had previous meetings and others not and whether this made a difference. To make sense of this Lefebvre argues that the rhythmanalyst, a participant wanting to understand the moment, pays attention to temporalities and their relations within wholes and gives an account of rhythms as the relation between present and presence. In this perspective, he thinks of time and space together. He is interested in the role space plays in our lives and argues that the rhythmanalyst should be capable of listening to a house, a street, a town, etc. (2019:33).  This approach means understanding the room, the speakerphones, the loud laughing as "things" which make themselves present and transforming them into presence by integrating them in an ensemble full of meaning (2019:33). Bringing the present into presence requires listening to immediate rhythms and combining them with what else is going on and might have been going on earlier. When I experienced myself having difficulties in finding my place and negotiating my interactions within the large group, I did not think that others might have the same difficulties and therefore did not take this into account. I paid no attention to how the spatial setting might have played a role in our interaction on the first day in the large group and how this was also a different space than the earlier meetings. It seems as if I was just caught up in my own struggle and did not see this a part of a whole, where negotiations of relations more generally might have been played out. The sense of tension in the room might not have been all about us, but what was emerging in the group.

In the narrative, one of the reflections at the meeting with the planning group was about the group of managers that did not seem to commit in the same way as other groups. At this meeting, we were able to explore our perceptions about this difference and one particular manager even questioned his role in this situation, since he still experienced resistance from the managers in his department. I shared with them my experience that some groups of professionals have a long history of working in isolation in their local institutions. They have traditionally been more closed towards other groups, which left us with an understanding that lack of will or engagement in this particular project was not the whole story about this group.

To change organisations and, e.g., demand a new way of collaboration, strong longstanding traditions and powerful patterns of interaction are questioned and challenged. Even when these participants seemed convinced that the new ways of collaborating across context were meaningful, it did not necessarily mean that they would know how to move on in new ways. Looking back, I now see this as a failure of research, since they did not know what was going on between them. Neither consultant nor colleague can ever understand the whole story or reasons for other people's ways of relating. However, the present curiosity that we found in this exploration seemed helpful in order to not just blame the managers for being resistant but to agree that we would just keep on inviting them.

Lefebvre's idea of rhythmanalysis helps us to understand how the role of a consultant is to juggle different identities that emerge – both concerning self and others – and respond to them in the present. Connected to Mead's ideas on gesture and response, selves are continuingly negotiated through interaction between self and others and therefore these processes become visible in the rhythms of, e.g., a leadership seminar. The gesturing and responding that emerge in the present moment helps us understand the patterns in time and space. Lefebvre brings me to acknowledge the need to pay attention to whatever ambiguities emerge in time and space and to engage with this. The temporal dimension also helps to understand how my anticipation of what kind of relationship I have had so far with a specific group of managers is always up for negotiation.  This fact emphasises again the need to pay attention to the present. We need to pay attention to these processes when identities are constantly negotiated with others, as I discovered in my experience in the narrative where my sense of self was paradoxically formed as both determinate and indeterminate.

Instead of wanting to rush the managers to be reflexive, I could have learned from Lefebvre´s argument for bringing the present rhythms into presence, which I take to mean staying with the meaning that arises in the present and orchestrate or respond to whatever drama that emerges. I see how my argument from my earlier presentation at the one-day seminars about how collaboration between managers from different departments would provoke different responses, disagreements and conflict might have been what happened in the large group. My own response to this was a feeling of disappointment and even irritation that the large group of managers did not speak up about this response, nor did they reflect on their interaction and support the overall idea with this process.  However, the idea of the consultant acting into the identity work of the managers must also include self-consciousness and reflexivity towards the identity work of him/herself.

Lefebvre brings me to revisit not only my understanding of organisational change but also our interactions in what he would call the rhythms of change. He states that there is no rhythm without both repetition and difference when arguing that *"when it concerns the everyday rites, ceremonies, fêtes, rules and laws, there is always something new and unforeseen that introduces itself into the repetitive: difference"* (2019:16). In my assignment in the narrative, the project aimed to change the way managers take responsibility from the individual – to a more shared responsibility for the collaboration across context in the work around young citizens. I relate this experience to what Lefebvre calls imprinting a rhythm on an era, about which he states that this kind of change or novelty will occasionally emerge to be seen a long time after the action (2019:24). Changing rhythms in who is talking to whom might or might not lead to this change, only time will tell.

Neither the consultant nor the manager can intervene from a detached position, as we ourselves are always involved, in order to help staff implement the necessary change, but can bring *"difference into the habitual patterning of interactions between people in the organisations into which they have been invited"* (Mowles, 2011:32). Helping managers make sense of what they are caught up with, might help make sense of their own habitual patterns of interaction or sensemaking towards the managers and staff in his department and through this relate to them in new ways. In this way, Lefebvre´s idea of paying attention to these social rhythms of change in order to reflect on them and reflexively orchestrate/interact with them might be one way of bringing difference into a group. The ongoing negotiations of my role and responsibility of the consultant is another element of the rhythm at the meeting in the large group, where I resist taking individual responsibility. However, my experience from the narrative shows how this is not my individual decision but an ongoing negotiation. Being aware of this power struggle as part of the rhythms helps me to find ways of engaging with it and in this way, bringing it into presence.

When thinking about organisational change as people imprinting a rhythm on an era, and in my narrative a new rhythm of collaboration across the previous structures or relations, Lefebvre has enabled me to think about pace in my assignments with expectations for the immediate results, which I often meet in working with leadership development. It occurs to me that the value of patience in processes of change is underestimated since the accelerated change seems to call for quick adaption. However, the reason I liked the particular assignment in this narrative was that we came to an understanding that the change they wanted would be an ongoing nonlinear process. That reasoning was also why we decided to continue to work together for at least a year. I see now that my experience of expectations about change with great speed from earlier assignments might have affected my focus on reflexivity as a tool that should be learned quickly.  In hindsight, I see that I got caught up in a wish for immediate signs of change already on the first day with the group despite the longer-term goal. When I judge how the managers are not reflexive in their conversations with each other, I find myself filled with fear of failure. Looking back, I was afraid to be judged as an incompetent and unhelpful consultant. However, my own judgement was based on an understanding of the consultant as enabling the managers to immediately change as a result of my interventions with the group.

Compared to the previous assignments at the one-day seminars, this more committed assignment for a year made me feel vulnerable and at risk of not being able to help them move together as they wished. The sense of freedom changed; the courage I found in the previous assignments to be rather provocative in order to challenge the habitual ways of thinking seemed to be constrained. I felt an enlarged demand to succeed and to "deliver" the change they wanted. By building a closer relation to the municipality, I seemed to lose the sense of freedom, which brings my attention to the potential reasons why the changing relationship came with a different kind of freedom.

When I think about the first one-day seminar, I was invited to present my perspective on their ideas about collaboration and coordination across contexts, after which we engaged in conversations. Planning the following leadership programme, I formulated a purpose and the methodological thinking about creating a culture of reflexivity that would help them to find new ways of collaborating. With Lefebvre, I have a theoretical and methodological approach for comparing the rhythms of leadership that emerged in the two one-day seminars compared to the meeting in the large group.


## Emergence of leadership

A wider exploration of the literature on leadership indicates what I have mentioned earlier in my P1, the understanding of leadership often based on a dichotomous perspective between the individual being and social process of becoming. Engaging with the question about how individuals can learn leadership is often referred to by arguing for a focus on either skillset or mindset.  There seems to be a pervasive argument that leadership is more about having or developing the right mindset and not as much about skillset (e.g., Kennedy et al., 2013 & Dweck, 2006). Other analysts emphasise the body in their phenomenological perspective on leadership, where our personal history, values and experiences are important to understand how leadership emerges (Küpers, 2013 & Ladkin, 2008). The becoming-perspective is strongly emphasised by social constructionists, where identity and leadership behaviour are constructed through dialogue and where the future is merely considered, and past and present plays a less significant role (e.g. Gergen, 2009 & Fairhurst & Grant, 2010).

Douglas Griffin criticises the dualistic focus on both individuals and social groups in the studies of leadership. He tries to overcome that dualism by introducing the perspective on the participative self-organisation. He argues that this perspective still preserves the contradiction between the individual and the collective but does so in a way that both entails the contradiction and transforms the relationship between the two.

Several of the contemporary texts I have read about leadership address the dualism between being and becoming and draw on the thinking of both individual and social group instead of thinking them as paradoxically interwoven as Griffin suggests. Küpers tries to overcome this problem and introduces integrative thinking through her presentation of be(com)ing, where leadership is interpreted as an embodied and relational practice (2013:340). A similar ambition is presented by Ladkin, who also takes an embodied perspective and combines this with an aesthetic and philosophical approach to leading beautifully, an aesthetic perspective on leadership, through which Ladkin refers to mastery, coherence and purpose as unconscious processes (2008). Despite the important contribution from these efforts to transcend the dualisms, I would argue that doing so by introducing embodiment and aesthetics as new themes are only replacing one dualism with new ones such as body-mind and conscious-unconscious.

Replacing one dualism with another seems to come with a risk of missing out on the nuances involved in the emergence of leadership. According to Alvesson & Kärremann, leadership theories are, however, often presented as idealised versions of reality and in seductive ways (2015:142). They argue that *"managers, management writers, and educators use leadership in an ideological way to promote their interests and, simultaneously, evoke a broad attribution of faith in positive forms of leadership leading to harmony, effectiveness, and moral order"* (ibid.). Alvesson even argues that leadership does not only deal with ambiguity but is an example of it and even produces it, which is not dealt with in much leadership literature (Alvesson & Sveningsson, 2003:965). Even theories that move away from the assumption of the heroic leader seems to address leadership as an idealised idea of doing good and therefore marginalise what is not-so-good.

Nevertheless, another critical approach to dualism in leadership literature is Collinson's approach to dialectics of leadership (2005). Regarding the problematic distinction between leaders and followers, he argues that it is of growing concern how dualistic perspectives prevent us from taking the blurry, multiple, ambiguous and contradictory character of power relations and identities into consideration. However, he claims that the exploration of how subjectivities are being negotiated could further enhance our understanding of leadership dialectics (2005:1435).

The perspective of Lefebvre gives a dialectical perspective on time and space and Antonacopoulou, who draws on Lefebvre's work, argues how this understanding of lived space emphasises the interdependency between being and becoming (2014:86) and helps to overcome the dualisms. Space must be understood as located in our actions as both a product and a producer which can also be seen in Lefebvre's understanding of present and presence. These perspectives mean that who and what we are is both a product of our being, while simultaneously produces what we are capable of becoming (ibid).

Even though Antonacopoulou is centering an argument for using this specific approach to understand the processes of learning, I find it very relevant to my work within leadership development as well as a way of understanding how leadership emerges and how to engage with this emergence as a facilitator.

## Freedom and organisational life

Regarding my animating question about the consequences of demands for change in leadership, Antonacopoulou also argues that space means freedom or liberation and emphasises how space is about freedom of movement and movement in space may well reflect freedom as a spatial fact (2014:87).

From my assumption that individuals are radically social, freedom is never something individually held, and leadership conduct is, therefore, not something we can freely choose individually. The rhythms in my relationship with the managers in this municipality changed from the first contact to the meeting in the large group. They showed more faith in me and wanted me to go on together with them, and as such, I felt more closely committed to them and their wishes. Their trust in my judgements about designing an iterative process for this leadership development programme based on ongoing reflexivity made me feel even more dependent in order for this to turn out as a success. Freedom emerges as such in processes of ongoing negotiation in the present.

Learning from Hegel's concept *of being with oneself in another,* as presented in my P3, I see now how the freedom I experienced was changing. I did not lose freedom, even though it felt like this, but as a consultant, I was both enabled and constrained in new ways because of my new relationship to this specific group. Developing closer relations to the group did not, in my experience in the narrative, seem to entail a space of liberation in itself.

Suddenly there was much more at stake since I planned an ongoing working relationship with the managers at the municipality, which seemed much more constraining.

Exploring freedom from a dialectical position, Bernstein takes a pragmatic position, including a paradoxical perspective on the individual and social in his understanding of freedom. He highlights how Arendt distinguishes between freedom and liberation (1983). The understanding of how liberation is always *from* something, whereas freedom *"is the positive achievement of human action and exists only as so long as that public space exists in which individuals debate together and participate with each other in determining public affairs"* (Bernstein, 1983:209). I take this to mean that freedom builds on the acknowledgement of our interdependency and is gained through ongoing conversations and participation with each other. When developing a closer connection with the managers in this municipality, it seems that my strong sense of self, and my courage to enter the room and face potential conflicts, comes under pressure. In order to live up to expectations about the helpful leadership development programme and my anticipation of expectations made me freeze for a moment.

However, understanding freedom, not as freedom *from* constraints, but as the freedom *to* engage with the changing ways of being both enabled and constrained, might lead to a sense of liberation. In hindsight, I see how my pattern of indeterminacy reoccurs. Sensing the anxiety in the room from the beginning and meeting the competing understandings of the consultant who should be in control, made my sense of self fragile. Even though this made it difficult to negotiate my ways into the smaller groups, I did not accept the invitation to take the responsibility alone.

When Honneth makes connections between processes of getting lost in others and suffering from indeterminacy, as presented in my P3, it makes sense to me in order to get a sense of either yourself or the others present. Most of the others present in my narrative did not express any expectations about fast progress, however I myself got lost in a more general understanding of what would be expected from the facilitator, and the suffering emerged in feeling both disappointed and stuck in the process. Afterwards, I felt disappointed with myself for responding in that way.

Lefebvre´s perspective on rhythmanalysis might help overcome the dualist approach to the emergence of leadership and understanding freedom. From a pragmatist perspective the *"application of dualisms, which are pairs of irreducible and excluding principles, precludes any understanding of the dynamics of processes because they cut through the very temporal continuities from which processes are constituted"* (Simpson & Marshall, 2010:354).  Instead of the dualistic perspective that I oppose, I suggest a paradoxical approach where *"one concept calls out for its opposite which is both defined and negated by it"* (Mowles, 2015:33). In this way, freedom is relationally negotiated as a way of acknowledging how the interdependency between people form ongoing possibilities to interact freely with the fact that we are paradoxically both enabling/disabling each other.

Dewey explains how freedom is not a metaphysical property people can possess, but that individuals can acquire freedom when developing new ways of relating to their own behaviour (Brinkmann, 2013:148). Paying attention to the changing rhythms concerning this group of managers might enable freedom for both the other participants and me.  We might gain detachment from our own involvement with the group and might find new ways of relating if we are able to share ongoing conversations about how we interdependently were both enabled and constrained at the same time. In this way, freedom means to engage in the present in which we are both enabled and constrained by time and space. Rhythmanalysis might help us get a strong and nuanced sense of ourselves and the subjectification processes we are constantly negotiating.

The paradox of detachment and involvement also leads me to think about the way we glorify change and freedom in our organisational life and through this disregard the fact that the emergence of leadership is not based on individual free choice. If learning and growth, as Dewey suggests, require participation in traditions and historically determined communities (Brinkmann, 2013:149), working within leadership development must address not only change but also the importance of tradition. When idealising change and freedom, in the rhythms in which we are engaged, one might lose the sense of the importance of tradition. When we do not pay attention to how we are constrained by tradition, it opens a space for thinking of others as being resistant to change and leads us to feeling stuck when trying to move on in new ways together. Antonacopoulou´s spatial perspective on liberation reflects an understanding of the fluidity of space (2014:87). The way I make sense of this is that Lefebvre´s understanding of space also is a way to overcome the dualisms.

Freedom, in this sense, is a way to interact with one another, acknowledging how we are all enabled and constrained in our ways of engaging and bringing these present different identities into the presence. To me, this means that freedom in leadership development programmes calls for space where all participants can show up as different individuals, enabled and constrained in different ways, recognising how being and becoming are both parts of the same process.

Lefebvre suggests that we only know whether a rhythm is slow or lively when comparing it to other rhythms. In my perspective, this raises the question as to how we can understand the current pace of change in an organisation and as to how the social rhythms are affected by the ongoing demand for organisational change? The focus on time makes me wonder how I can understand the demand for a pace that I find myself caught up in, in my narrative, when experiencing an urgent demand for reflexivity? Lefebvre developed his thinking at the beginning of the 20th century and engaged with Hegel, Marx, Nietzsche, Heidegger, Sartre and many more, which makes him difficult to classify. Nevertheless, although his ideas have been brought into organisational studies, exploring topics such as leadership, power, politics (Kingma, Dale & Wassermann, 2018:12), continuity is neglected. However, how can we bring his rhythmanalysis into a contemporary understanding of time and space in order to understand the traditions in which we are involved?

## Social acceleration as a contemporary perspective on leadership development

With Lefebvre's focus on time, I have become aware of the ambitious approach to the time pressure I seem to bring into the assignment in the narrative. I felt a sense of urgency in order to make a change in the organisation. Exploring the understanding of pace in order to inquire further into the negotiations of professional identities in the field of leadership development brings me to the German sociologist Hartmut Rosa.

Like Lefebvre, Rosa is inspired by Hegel and takes a dialectic perspective. Rosa analyses the consequences of what he describes as social acceleration and forms a theory about modernity. He argues that *"The social formation of modernity is defined structurally by the fact that it is capable only of dynamic stabilisation, while its cultural program is aimed at systematically increasing the share of the world of both individuals and cultures"* (2019:308). This perspective is based on his understanding that basic institutions of society, including public welfare organisations, in which my work is carried out, are only capable of reproducing themselves in a mode of escalation (ibid). What he argues is the existence of an ongoing increase in pace, or one might say that the rhythms, continue to reflect an enormous urgency. Rosa presents three categories of acceleration, namely technological acceleration, the acceleration of social change, and an acceleration in the pace of life (2010:16). He states that to maintain stability, we must all move faster and faster, and this pace then becomes the new normal to which we compare and judge the next movement.

Rosa argues that the consequences of this acceleration lead to alienation, understood as *a relation of relationlessness* described as the kind of relationship where *"subject and world confront each other with indifference or hostility and thus without any inner connection"* (2019:184). This definition refers to a state where the world appears cold, rigid, repulsive and non-responsive and a state where the pace is fast, and people cannot keep following the track.

This brings my attention to the possible dangers we also face in leadership development processes, such as the one I am engaged in with this group of managers. Differences in the group based on when the participants were included in this process and how they belong to other groups with different traditions and history comes with the risk of alienation. If we rush others and do not spend time trying to listen and understand these differences and instead get caught up in a wish for speed in the change we desire, we might achieve the exact opposite of what we aim for. My own experience of feeling dissatisfied immediately with the conversations in the group, and my wish for reflexivity, could be seen as a step on the way to losing my relationship with the participants. Even though I wrote down all the suggestions for topics for the next meeting in detail, I was unable to take them in and found myself hostile towards them since I thought they were incompatible with the process I had in mind. Only afterwards, when I could relate to the suggestions from a more detached position, and even further in reflections with the planning group, I rediscovered an openness and a curiosity towards making sense of the suggestions and taking them into account.

In Rosa´s way of perceiving our relationship with the world, he states that even very different scholarly perspectives on the successful relationship to the world, such as Habermas, Honneth and Jaeggi, agree that *"...various individually and historically manifested ways in which human beings relate to the world are controlled and determined only to a small extent – and in many respects not at all – by individuals themselves, and instead are shaped and predetermined by social conditions that all arise, solidify, and change behind their backs"* (2019:27). With this perspective, Rosa does not only suggest potential alienation in our relation to the world, but he also points to the fact that we might risk being alienated from our body, as a thing or an instrument or pure resource (2019:104). In order to maintain growth, innovation and acceleration, humans need to find energy as, e.g. motivation, since they *must* continuingly put in more energy in order to maintain their competitiveness for keeping their place or position (ibid). This perspective reinforces the experience in the narrative, where I seem to think that we were expected to show a rapid movement or development in the large group, without anyone having expressed such demands.

Even though Rosa´s analysis does not specifically concern the workplace but addresses human experience more generally in relation to the world, his arguments seem to apply to the workplace as well. When we experience an acceleration in change, and we meet ongoing new expectations and demands for us to change and learn, it might come along with strong emotional responses. The tension I sensed already when the participants entered the room at the meeting in the large group seemed to me as a sign that we were all emotionally at work trying to find our ways into this group.

## Emotional labour and identity work in rhythms of change

Many scholars, with early inspiration from Hochschild (1983), address that everyday work life, in general, requires emotional labour. This point raises attention to the emotional dissonance, or tension one can experience when meeting expectations of what is considered appropriate emotions in the workplace (O´Brien & Linehan, 2018:1). However, rather than addressing a conflict between an authentic self and an organizationally mandated display of appropriate emotions, and in this way pointing to a gap between selves at work and natural selves as the original emotional labour literature did, the understanding of emotional dissonance can also be perceived as the *"challenges in reconciling competing emotion and identity possibilities that surface in a given context"* (O´Brien & Linehan, 2018:19).

This perspective challenges the idea of authenticity and critiques the understanding that emotion is more authentic before it enters organisational life and is transformed to adapt to organisational ends and becomes inauthentic. The argument can also be seen as overcoming a dualism and also includes a critique of the idea of authenticity since this understanding *"ignore the idea of multiple identities that are simultaneously salient and do not account for the evidence that dissonance and 'faking' can be tolerated and at times result in positive employee outcomes"* (O´Brien & Linehan, 2018:2).

In my argument for a paradoxical relation between the individual and the social group, it makes sense to understand how individual identities are continually negotiated in relations to others. As a contrast to Rosa´s slightly (at times) limited belief in individual control or determination in relation to the world (2019:27), my understanding recognises individual agency more fully. The freedom to act is not based on an understanding of individuals not being constrained but out of an understanding of interdependence between humans that is both enabling and disabling at the same time. Freedom in this perspective concerns the making of individual judgements about the way we engage with the fact that we are both enabled and constrained at the same time. The idea of alienation might be both a result, and a risk, of losing the paradox of individual and social. The increased pace and demand for fast change might in itself encourage idealisations and, through these, alienation.

Combined with my understanding from my P2, that we are all embedded in power relations and game-playing when entering the realm of organisations, this means that meeting in this new group might be a threat to their identity as managers for their area and require identity work in order to find out who they can be in this social setting and how this can fluctuate with their sense of self in other relations.  In this understanding, negotiations of identity are both going on in relation to self and others and come with a risk of alienation. The loud laughing during the day of the first meeting in the large group might have been a sign of anxiety and tension when dealing with emotional dissonance and identities at work.

I also felt myself emotionally at work, e.g. when trying to find out how to relate to the small groups and resisting the invitation to accept the role of the responsible consultant without turning the participants against me. I was afraid of what they would think of me and that they would not engage in the collaboration with me. The invitation to take this position of the consultant surprised me as it was different from my earlier experiences in this group. This phenomenon made me anxious and confused about my sense of self as a consultant.  At this time, I was trying to find my feet and to be both part of the group but not a participant equally with the others, which I found difficult. It also made me respond to the participants differently compared to the earlier meetings since my more provocative and straightforward sharing of opinions were held back.  This point might indicate an elusive character or maybe just a more fluent understanding of my sense of self when I move from thinking of myself as part of the group. At the same time, I am reminded of how I am not an equal part, with the emotional dissonance that comes along with navigating between these two positions or ways of understanding myself. With this example, it becomes clear how identity is not a thing individually held, but a process of ongoing negotiations with others which require attention and identity work.

When acceleration also increases in the way we try to change organisations, we might lose the sense of the emotional work and the way our identities are continuingly negotiated, simply because we do not spend enough time paying attention to these processes. In the narrative, we were not able to detach ourselves from the emotional experiences on the day of the meeting to reflect on them together. I found that easier afterwards and even more helpful when sharing those reflections with the planning group. The insights coming out of these retrospective reflections might or might not lead to a more detached position in the next meeting with the large group.

Simpson & Marshall argue that there is a very little room for emotional experiences, as experienced in the narrative, in the rational problem-solving and decision-making organisational context in which learning processes take place (2010:352). They indicate that shame, embarrassment, disappointment, and humiliation come with the experience of failure that might be related to processes of learning and that the influence of learning on emotions is largely ignored (2010:352). Vince, however, points out how our understanding of emotions in organisations in recent years has become enhanced but argues that the role of the unconscious has not been illuminated (2019:953). Baldwin argues that not only are we cognitive and emotional beings, but we need theories of habitual action in order to deal better with the less deliberate facets of human conduct to complement the overly cognitive perspective (1988:36). Based on Mead's understanding of gesture and response as presented in my P3, emotions arise, from a pragmatic perspective, e.g., when there is a difference between our anticipation and the actual response it calls out. The emotion can be seen as like any other gesture that constitutes an action (Simpson & Marshall, 2010:357).

In my narrative, this point brings attention to my understanding of the leadership development process, aiming for reflection and reflexivity in the group. Based on my experience from the two one-day seminars, where reflexive conversations just emerged, I did not expect the interaction in the large group to be fundamentally different. When the managers responded with simple answers about the best solutions to enable collaboration with no focus on their own patterns of behaviour, I experienced disappointment and frustration. I found myself withdrawing from the conversation, just listening and writing the comments in my notebook. Based on my earlier experience with several of the managers, I was not prepared for them to be unable to engage in critical reflexivity.  I was surprised, and that made me feel stuck.

Mead understands emotional, habitual, and conscious processes as being integrated (Baldwin, 1988:53). He understands habits as both rather simple responses to stimuli, but also that habit can take more complex forms when, e.g. being linked together. He writes, *"I have referred just now to the relationship of the substance as reflected in the body of habits, to the varied responses answering to the attributes. … We have here a relationship of dependence of one response on another…"* (Mead, 1934:126). Habits can be performed unconsciously when they are well-learned (Baldwin, 1988:42) and Mead argues that *"the structure of society lies in these social habits, and only in so far as we can take these social habits into ourselves can we become selves"* (1936:375). Related to my narrative, I take this to mean that when I do not feel sympathetic towards the way the conversations turned out, nor the suggested idea of an information system; I fail to recognise what might be a strong habitual pattern in the group as to how to approach such situations and my own habitual pattern of responding to that.

If we are alienated from our self and others, we do not relate or respond, which leaves us without the social self-consciousness we need in the processes of renegotiation of identity, which leads me back to Rosa.


## Resonance and radical openness to self and others

Rosa´s first interest in linking human relations to time and his perspective on acceleration led him to think about how our problematic relation to time might also mean that something is wrong with our relation to the world (Rosa & Endres, 2017). With a presumption of this connection, Rosa turns to his understanding of resonance and offers a solution to the problematic consequences of social acceleration. Drawing on both Mead and Merleau-Ponty, as I also do in my P3, he argues how neither identity nor sociality is possible in the absence of experiences of responsiveness (2019:171).

Further, he argues that human beings desire resonant relationships, which existentially shape us. In response to the risk of alienation, he introduces and advocates for the concept of resonance in order to understand an ideal relationship with the world around us. Resonance from Rosa´s perspective is not to be understood as consonance or harmony, just as he underlines that dissonance does not mean alienation (2019:184). Resonance is when we are both moved by the world and moving it at the same time. Rosa highlights the Hegelian perspective on how subject and world interpenetrate while permeating both sides, which, according to Rosa, holds on to the mystery in terms of Hegel´s "world-spirit" (2019:316). Losing this mystery has reduced our perception of humans and nature and the relationship between them and turned them into instruments and resources.

Relating this to the narrative, I recognise how my way of relating to the managers on the day of the first meeting in the large group was somehow instrumentalising them. I had recommended a specific way of working emphasising managers to engage in reflexivity in order to enable change. I expect that this way of working was familiar to the participants as well and, from the same perspective, their response might have been understood as resistance. My insecurity about whether reflexivity would actually make a difference and the fact that reflexivity did not even emerge in the first meeting, made me anxious, which I shamefully see now made me wish for them to do as they were told. Thankfully, the response from the large group, my following silent conversations with myself and the shared reflections with the planning group, made me see my own patterns of consultant behaviour.

Rosa argues that our interaction with the world and each other more and more reminds us of a chamber of echoes, in which we only hear our own voices, which leaves us lonely, alienated and with a sense of emptiness. With resonance, he introduces a way of relation, where we engage in communities based on listening and responding despite the competition, as he sees competition as a key structural element in modernity that might lead to alienation (2019:21).

If leadership development programmes and consulting within these processes are to make any impact at all, we need to strive for resonance in the relations within which we engage. As facilitators, we might or might not enable others to listen to each other, neither is it in our control to secure resonance; however, facilitators could be highly influential in making it more or less likely.

Looking back, I see how my narrative is an example of everybody talking from their own perspective, having their mouths full of words and maybe not listening carefully enough to each other. The push and pulls on identities in leadership programmes, like the one my narrative evokes, might also come with the risk of participants being unable to relate to more than our own emotional response. Since the emotional aspects were not recognised much at the meeting in the large group, the risk of alienation might have been intensified. We might better have been able to recognise each other, to resonate with each other in undertaking the task if we had been able to address the emotional reactions and to share them.

Rosa emphasises a certain way of relating to both ourselves and each other. In order to avoid contributing to an increase in the acceleration of our own change in identity, and through this get lost in oneself or others, we must also both remain stable and open to change at the same time. When we experience dissonance concerning ourselves or others, the idea of resonance can be connected to Bernstein's perspective on radical openness towards the otherness of others. We can recommend that humans investigate both strangeness and familiarity of what is other and alien from a position of the doubt instead of the position of certainty (Mowles, 2012: 552). Bernstein describes radical openness as the ability to hold on to our beliefs while at the same time, staying dynamically open. In this sense, it is important to restate how there is no dichotomy between resonance and dissonance, but rather dissonance can be a natural part of a resonant relation.

This insight places new responsibilities on the self because it means accepting our own fallibility and taking this seriously. Taking it seriously means, in this perspective, that we do not suppress the otherness of others, but willingly listen and maybe seek mutual, reciprocal understanding (Bernstein, 1991:337). Through this insight, the foundation of our identity *"is a fragile and temporary achievement that can always be ruptured by unexpected contingencies"* (ibid).

What I experienced in the narrative is that the participants were not radically open to otherness; none of us seems to inquire much into the differences between us but move on into the conversations holding on to our own beliefs. I was caught up in my own anxiety and my sense that we were not going in the right direction together, which made me worry. I did not offer them my expertise on how to change their ways of working together but wanted to help them gain a reflexive detachment about their ways of interacting in order to enable change. In hindsight, I see how negotiations of roles in the room were not openly discussed and how this might have constrained us to relate openly to the otherness of each other.

However, the insecurities we experienced made the present room full of tension, with no time to explore this.

Only some of the participants had met the consultant before and those who had not may have expected a more traditional consultant offering them exact knowledge on what to do or at least offer interventions which could lead to change in a certain way. Instead, I presented a programme in which I would participate in reflexive dialogues about shared experiences with each other. Looking back, I come to think that some of the managers might have found it strange and unfamiliar to be in this kind of relation to a consultant and the other managers. I had the feeling that they wanted to position me as being the person responsible for the process and maybe the kind of consultant with whom they were more familiar. I, on the other hand, held on to my idea of not wanting to present any kind of solutions, even though I had come to think of reflexivity as the solution. Only afterwards, I was able to see how we had neglected the otherness of each other. We had not spent enough time getting to know one another in order for me to make judgements about how we might, in time, enable a reflexive community. Getting to know one another is not only about an extended presentation process. With this perspective it is about a constant focus and the continuing allocation of time to reveal our complex entangled pressures, desires, aspirations, histories etc. in order to build relationships where we might or might not experience resonance. I also see how I turned reflexivity into a tool that should provide us with a specific result, such as new culture and new ways of collaborating. Instead of paying attention to the present and, as Lefebvre suggests, orchestrating the presence with whatever emerged, I was already occupied with the future and where this could or would take us.

In situations where we meet unfamiliar or even alien responses from others, the renegotiation of our own identity comes with multiple insecurities since the negotiation of our identity is related to others' judgements and validation of our identity, and with Mead's perspective (1934:176), our own anticipation of these others' evaluations.

Studying academics at work, Knights and Clarke argue that identity and insecurities are conceptually important to the study of organisations (2014:336) and argue that feelings of insecurity tend to generate a preoccupation with stabilising our identity. Rosa's perspective on the accelerating contingent nature of the world challenges this sense of stability, which again reinforces the insecurity, which we expect identity to dissipate (ibid). One of the arguments in Knights and Clarke's study, where they explore insecure identities working in academia, and especially at business schools, is that *"conforming to the demands of excessive audits and assessments aggravates insecurities about the existential meaning of what we do, possibly distancing us from the community that we otherwise seek to impress"* (2014:352). This consideration might explain the change in rhythm from the first two one-day seminars to where all I had to do was to make a presentation of my views on developing a shared responsibility and collaboration across contexts upon which for them to reflect. When planning the process for the next year, we suddenly had formulated goals such as, e.g., developing a culture of reflexivity. This list made me feel insecure and question my own achievements. I was uncertain about whether we could perform in the ways we had planned.

Working at a University College myself might have affected my way of perceiving my role since I have also experience how audits etc. have become an increasing part of my job. So even if there were no specific goals formulated or assessments from the Municipality, I brought in pressures from assessments experienced in other assignments.  I was preoccupied with these future goals, which prevented me from being closely connected with the managers and the emotional and habitual responses they were expressing.

I did not explore the suggestion about an information system providing the managers with knowledge about different employees and their different tasks or how this might be helpful to them. Instead, I was faced with my own beliefs about how that kind of knowledge is not the only solution and how this would not help us in developing a reflexive community which was part of the goal in this process. Only later I did so, in my preparations before the next meeting. In my investigation with the planning group, I did realise how the wish for knowledge can express that they were struggling with uncertainty and a need for more solid ground to find new ways of interacting.  I see how I was speeding up the process in order to achieve my own goals to reduce my uncertainty towards the effect on the reflexive process. Through this process, I see that there is a tendency not to acknowledge the emotional and habitual elements in processes of leadership development.

Bernstein emphasises the importance of holding on to our beliefs while remaining open to others and that the experience of otherness can both concern others and ourselves. Our personal work within these processes might be worth paying even more attention to than most consultants and scholars do when working within or writing about leadership development. When thinking of our work life as an ongoing arena for identity work, this offers possibilities of bringing attention to identity struggles in leadership development programmes, like the one in my narrative, as a way of taking these processes seriously. It is suggested by Hay how uncomfortable surfacing struggles, which are often silenced, may resonate with managers in other contexts and be helpful in order to demonstrate insecurity and the central element of becoming a manager (2014:521-522).

In my narrative, I experience how it is easier for both me and Albert to share our doubts and insecurities in the planning group. It was also easier for me when I attended the earlier workshops and did not have the same degree of performance measures defined, and the group was smaller. However, it is also my experience that sharing your own beliefs or doubts, and maybe even the emotional dissonance you experience, and listening closely to these experiences of others might be relevant in leadership development programmes. The idea of showing your own vulnerability, and maybe disturbing the social understanding of the competent heroic consultant, brings my attention back to finding the courage to do so – also, in the case of my narrative, in the large and new group.

As a consultant, I would like to enable resonance and reflexivity, and the one thing I might be able to do is to bring in my own ghosts, share my own struggles with the group by expressing my own habitual patterns and emotional reactions and in this way maybe enable others to do the same. I have begun to do this more in different situations of my job, both with co-workers and clients. Doing this comes with the risk of being rejected or misjudged, which then again is also part of the struggles I might be able to share with the people with whom I work.

At the same time, I acknowledge the interdependency of others and the fact that I am also both enabled and constrained in time and space to do so. Paying attention to my own ways of engaging with freedom into these power dynamics, and even starting conversations about this, might lead to reducing the constraints, so that resonance and reflexivity become more of a possibility for others.

## Summing up

Exploring my experience of rhythms of change in my working with leadership development in a Danish municipality supports my understanding that movements in identities are not only complex processes but also an essential element of my work. The perspective on organisational rhythms, inspired by Lefebvre, has helped to address the complexity of processes of negotiating identity, and how our understanding of change should be closely connected to repetition and that these should not be seen as opposites.

In general, I argue against thinking or getting stuck in dualisms. We might need dualisms to think with, but we should not just oscillate between them. We do not need to choose but need to understand the processes that allows us to navigate paradoxes. Holding on to dichotomy reduces our understanding of the complexity of organisational life. Instead, I argue further that the acceleration of pace, that Rosa explains, has hugely influenced my way of working within leadership development programmes and that this leads to a risk of alienation in my relation to the people I work with and among them as well. In my narrative I have explained how the speed and the strong focus on the goal came with the risk of instrumentalising the people involved in these processes and an alienation from both ourselves and others. I argue that we must pay closer attention to tradition, habits and emotions as central elements in the emergence of leadership and that doing so demands a specific way of relating. When experiencing dissonance and contradictory emotions, or meeting unexpected habitual responses, which could be interpreted as resistance, these responses should be recognised and considered necessary to orchestrate into presence. I see how we seem to idealise an individual perspective on freedom when we think that humans can change or become another version of themselves, if only they realise and are motivated by the necessity of doing so.

In my understanding of freedom, not as freedom *from*, but the freedom *to,* the interdependence between people is acknowledged. Freedom then is about the way we engage with being both enabled and constrained at the same time; our way of relating to each other should be based on openness to otherness since different people are enabled and constrained in different ways. Listening to others and gaining detachment from our involvement through reflexive dialogues might still be one way of doing this, however not in an instrumentalised way or as a goal in itself. This project reinforces the importance of being with oneself in another. In my perspective, a resonant relationship to the world depends upon this paradoxical understanding of the individual and social. By taking the attitude of both self and others, we might find the freedom to accept and engage with ourselves and others and the interdependency between us.

Working as a consultant, I must relate to the interaction that I am involved with at the time, and instead of looking to manage and control what should be going on, I should recognise my own emotional and habitual reactions and maybe even share them with others. However, if being human also means that we never know in advance whatever will emerge, e.g., in processes of leadership development, and that we will experience unexpected responses in both ourselves and others, we must always be prepared to be surprised. The consequences of our experience with other people become part of who we are. Since we never know the consequences in advance, the ongoing inquiry into making sense of what happens is thus important for our sense of self and others.

If we engage more with what emerges in the room, instead of being preoccupied with controlling the future outcomes or what other people might think of us, it might affect the possibility of resonance and developing close relationships instead of being alienated from either ourselves or others. However, we should be cautious to not turn resonance nor reflexivity into new management tools, instead of being concerned with whatever emerges in the present.  We must also recognise that future orientation, the need for quick changes and for managing other people´s impressions of us, are also part of the political game going on in organisations – we have to engage with this game and understand that resonance and reflexivity might or might not emerge and cannot be controlled.

The role of the facilitator must be based on a strong sense of self and others, which means taking a position based on individual identity and recognising that this position can only be good enough for now, emerging as both repetitive and different at the same time through processes of negotiation. Freedom in this perspective is to engage in close, both enabling and constraining, relations with both self and others and to share participation and conversation, which might or might not result in resonance or liberation.

# Synopsis of research

## Introduction

In this thesis, I have inquired into the processes of negotiating identity within the various assignments I work on as an associate professor at the University College of Copenhagen. Whether I am teaching, facilitating, coaching, or counselling students, clients, or co-workers, my work always engages in leadership processes – mostly through my collaboration with leaders and through my own temporary leadership during consultancies. When leading, I find myself and others endeavour to find agency in the ongoing situations we are engaged in and find ourselves entangled in relationships with others. This observation has led me to explore how the struggle for freedom is played out in the identity work involved within the practice of leadership in everyday organizational life.

In this thesis, I seek to explore the struggles for freedom within leadership practices by focusing on the emerging selves involved in leadership in my everyday organizational life.  Even though management studies in this field are still mostly inspired by a behavioristic perspective on individuals, focusing on personal skills, etc., studies of the self have moved away from the essentialist and context-independent approach, acknowledging the self as being entangled with sociocultural contexts and emphasizing the self as being intrinsically interwoven with them (Stetsenko & Arievitch, 2004:475). My research is critical towards how scholarship tends to focus merely on dichotomic perceptions of individuals and their relation to social systems or structures (Collinson, 2005, Alvesson & Svenningsson, 2003, Fairhurst,

2001). The emphasis seems to be on how leadership can impact the organization, whereas leadership is seen as unaffected by the organization. I argue, however, how this must be replaced by a paradoxical understanding of individual and social as mutually constitutive. Understanding freedom in the processes of negotiating identities must consider, therefore, how the individual and social are continuingly and mutually constituted. Losing this paradox comes with the risk of alienation from oneself or others. My claim is that by taking the interdependency between people seriously, we might experience some sense of freedom and avoid a collapse in our sense of agency in everyday leadership practice. Working with leaders and perceiving my own practice as ongoing situations of temporary leadership, which I will explain further in this synopsis, my research explores how we can understand the continuing enabling and constraining involved with everyday leadership practice, and through this find agency. Thus, my inquiry is based on the assumption that organisational life is about human interaction and the interweaving of intentions (Stacey & Mowles, 2016:316).

Based on the arguments in the four projects, the purpose of this synopsis is to look back on the findings and iteratively to engage with them in another reflexive turn. On this basis, I formulate the final arguments and contributions to knowledge and practice. The content of this synopsis consists of an account of the methodological perspectives on which my research relies and explains the methods I have used as a result of my way of thinking about these choices. Further, I will reflect on the ethics involved in the research process. Additionally, the synopsis will present summaries of each project supplemented with new reflections based on my present perspective and further inquiry, which draw on insights from the other projects and, in some instances, on new literature. Each project in the thesis has been presented as originally written and has not been revised afterwards. The projects express the iterative research process and ongoing refinement of my arguments as they emerge during the process of writing the projects. This process leaves me with the opportunity to reflect on the major themes and provides the reader and me with an insight into how my thinking has moved on during the research process. This synoptic process aims to reflect on the development in my thinking over the time I have been engaged in this research and develop and present arguments and contributions, to both knowledge and practice, of this thesis.

As such, *"the complex responsive processes research method leads to a research account that tracks its own actual development as further reflexivity"* (Stacey & Griffin, 2005:25), which is a requirement for all students on the DMan programme. In continuation of this approach, every student is required to explicitly account for both contributions to practice and knowledge in the thesis.

## Research theme

Taking various positions over time as a teacher, conversation partner, consultant, facilitator, and researcher to contribute to leadership processes in the Danish welfare sector, I have been puzzled about the unpredictability and complexity involved in these processes and the identity struggles that come along with them.  Expectations within these different roles and the interplay between the different intentions with which other people and I interact in everyday organizational life have led me to understand organisations similarly to Stacey and Mowles when they perceive organisations as unpredictable emergence of order in disorder (2016:316). Working with others then means the continuous experience of recognising ourselves and others as social individuals forming and being formed by each other in everyday interactions.

My initial research interest was about how the people I work with and I are interrelated as social beings and how we can maintain a sense of individuality within these social processes of being and becoming who we are. This theme has emerged and developed through an iterative process of doing this research and led me to my research theme:

*An inquiry into the paradoxical and contradictory experience of freedom and constraint within the social process of negotiating leadership identity.*

This theme has evolved throughout the whole research process. Iteratively, and as a result of collaborative processes with others, I have developed my way of thinking about my research, and through this iterative process, my research has emerged. In the following sections, I will present how these processes have formed the methodological ground for my research.


## Approach to research methodology

As a student in the Doctor of Management (DMan) programme, I am part of a research community where we are encouraged to engage with the perspective of complex responsive processes of relating and the various theories that influenced it. This perspective was originally developed by Ralph Stacey, Doug Griffin, and Patricia Shaw and has emerged from insights based on group analytical thinking inspired by Foulkes, complexity sciences, process sociology of Norbert Elias, and pragmatic philosophy as developed by Mead and Dewey (as explained further by Mowles, 2017). From the perspective of complex responsive processes of relating, the subject and object of a research process are always inseparable. Stacey argues that the complex responsive processes perspective is an action theory, a temporal process theory in which it does not make sense to separate the individual and the social in terms of *"inside or outside, above or below, in front or behind"* (2003:120). Subjects form and are formed by the object, which makes the researcher and the researched paradoxically related. I take this paradoxical approach to my research and draw primarily on the sociological and pragmatist aspects in this thesis.

Inspired by Elias, Mowles (who is also part of the community influenced by and influencing the perspective of complex responsive processes of relating) argues that a dualistic approach to subjectivity and objectivity is unhelpful and that researchers are both involved and detached at the same time (Mowles, 2015, 2015a), so striving for objectivity can be understood as a process instead of a position. Therefore, in my research, the projects focus on my practice and the interplay between people in my work life. The way I make sense of my involvement with others in these experiences is formed by my ongoing involvement, i.e., with my co-workers in the DMan community, and thus continuously forming my interpretation in new ways. Thinking of the researcher and any social actor as social through and through (Stacey, 2003:120), my research methods encourage a striving for detachment to my involvement, however, recognizing that I can never gain an entirely detached perspective.

The method recommended for doctoral researchers at the DMan is "that of taking one´s own experience seriously to reflexively explore the complex responsive processes of human relating" (Stacey & Mowles, 2016:509). This process means paying attention to what goes on in our everyday lived experiences with other people in our work life. The genesis of my inquiry is to investigate situations in my everyday work life, where I reflexively explore breakdowns in my practice. Inspired by pragmatist ideas of e.g. John

Dewey, the approach to my inquiry relies on the key assumption that qualitative research is closely connected to practice and occurs in situations of breakdowns, as Brinkmann suggests: *"The main idea in breakdown-oriented research is that researchers should frame situations of breakdowns as a mystery, which is a first step towards resolving the breakdown"* (2012:44).

My inquiry into experiences of breakdowns, i.e., a situation where I feel stuck in my interactions or unable to make sense of what is going on in my practice, can be revealing material and thus the ground for understanding everyday organizational life and entering into fruitful interpretations of significant cultural issues (Brinkmann, 2012:86). From a pragmatist perspective, knowing is intimately connected to doing, and the goal of this research process is, therefore, to act in specific situations (ibid, 2014:722). Therefore, these situations from my work experience can be seen as the data for my analysis in this thesis. My understanding is that data is not something "given" that a researcher can collect, but always "taken" since it is produced, constructed, and mediated by human activities (ibid:721).

The theories I draw on are, to some extent, inspired by those we are encouraged to engage with on the DMan. However, we do not need to agree with these perspectives, and my thesis is also based on other theories, e.g. Merleau- Ponty (1968), Lefebvre (2019), and Rosa (2019). The choice of theories emerges primarily from the topics in the breakdowns. I inquire into finding insights that help me make sense of what is going on for me and others. Furthermore, the strong inspiration from the perspective of complex responsive processes of human relating, process sociology, and pragmatist philosophy does not prevent me from looking into more widespread and commonly expressed ideas within management and organisational studies. This effort helps me form my own stance to clarify with which perspectives I agree and which I will be critical towards. The essential theories in this thesis are closely connected to the breakdown-oriented research process, studying experiences of stumbling in our everyday lives (Brinkmann, 2014:724) to regain a sense of agency. The choice of theories is based on a wide range of readings that are brought in because they help me understand the strangeness of the world (ibid). In this way, the theories I draw on have emerged iteratively. However, the scholars I have found most helpful share the Hegelian arguments against dualisms and put an emphasis on paradoxes.

## Participation and collaboration on the DMan Programme

As a student at the DMan doctorate programme, I have become part of a community that also means joining a set of traditions, norms, and expectations about research. One of the core themes in the processes involved in the research on the DMan is the understanding of research not as merely a subjective inquiry but more of a collaborative process, as described further below. This approach resonates with my initial understanding of the researcher as social through and through, as mentioned above, and has been essential in my efforts in gaining detachment from my own involvement in the processes into which I inquire. The collaborative approach can be conflictual because my understandings have been contested by others, and dissonance has emerged. The conflicting ideas and understanding have been explored and helped me gain detachment from my own perceptions and find ways of moving on in my practice at work. Thus, the research can still be considered as my individual work based on my individual choices and perspectives, however without the dichotomic understanding of the subject and object toward which I, as presented earlier, was critical from the beginning of my research process.

All doctoral students and members of faculty meet at residentials four times a year over four days. During residentials, faculty members (or occasionally guest lecturers) make presentations on themes related to the students´ research theoretically and methodologically. Based on these inputs and common readings before each residential, we reflect together on the themes taken up in both the large community and smaller groups and how the presented ideas make sense to us in different or similar ways.

For the duration of the doctorate, students at all stages of their doctorate join pre-existing learning sets with a first supervisor and three fellow students, which means that most learning sets have students at different stages of their doctorate. At the residentials, there are several meetings in the learning set, during which we discuss our experience at the residential and the work of each individual doctoral student in the set. In the learning set, we comment in writing on each other's work as it is written and join in conversations about the responses to the comments when we meet. Each set repeats this way of working together at virtual meetings six weeks after the residential. In this way, we commit to producing new writing, receive detailed comments on our writing, research theme, method and arguments from our first supervisor (and occasionally the second supervisor) and fellow students in the learning set, and continue ongoing discussions about research projects when we meet. Due to Covid 19 restrictions, my last four residentials were virtual, which seemed to constrain the informal conversations we share over dinner, at the coffee machine, etc. I found it more difficult to relate to the new colleagues I did not meet in person because we did not engage in informal conversations between sessions in the larger community. Building relationships with newcomers or staying in relation with fellow students greatly impacted the collaborative approach at the DMan, which seemed constrained when we were unable to meet physically. Simultaneously, connecting virtually with the community enabled some of us to set up virtual meetings in between residentials with others who are not in the learning set. I enjoyed these as they seemed to make it up for some of the conversations on which we missed out. In this sense, the Covid 19 restrictions were at the same time constraining and enabling the collaboration at the DMan, while also revealing the unusual way this professional doctorate programme is organised.

Additionally, we share discussions with a second supervisor and the wider DMan community. The second supervisor comments at least one time on each project with written comments or suggestions about new considerations. At each residential, different students present their work and receive responses from the other students (usually at least 20) and six faculty members.

Every morning at the residentials, we have a community meeting for one and a half hours with no agenda. Inspired by group analysis practice, we sit in a large circle, and both faculty members and students are encouraged to speak freely about what they want to share with the group and the way we work together. The meeting can be seen as an experiential group (Mowles, 2017:8), with members reflecting on what is going on in the group. Anxiety-provoking themes tend to emerge continually, such as the question of being good enough to finish the doctorate. We discuss what patterns seem to emerge in our group and how we respond to each other in shared conversations. However, we also draw parallels to organizational life from our shared experiences. These conversations about, e.g., power struggles, inclusion and exclusion processes, or leadership help us understand what is going on between other people and us. In addition to the ongoing conversations in the set and with the larger community, these meetings also help us gain detachment in our ways of being involved and explore the patterning within groups. Such new insights are also drawn into the research in making sense of what is going on for myself and other people in my practice. One example is my experience of our learning set not claiming as much time to talk about ourselves in the large group, compared to some of the other sets. This observation made us reflect on how the conversations in the wider community were often about emotional drama and how our set did not find ourselves caught up in such magnified dramatic processes to the same extent and, therefore, in some instances, unable to speak as much. These reflections also made me realize my own pattern of not feeling comfortable about speaking too much about myself and how I found myself judgmental towards other people, who, in my perspective, were claiming too much time in the large group.

On a smaller scale, these kinds of reflections are continued in the learning set and the more informal groups when we meet in, e.g., coffee breaks. In the beginning, I found it quite difficult to find my voice in the large group. Since I am not usually hesitant in speaking up, and because my learning set made me reflect on my silence, I was puzzled by my way of engaging at these community meetings. We talked about how our learning set had developed a different and quieter way of handling drama than what we experienced from the other groups at the community meetings. We did not seek as much attention in situations of heightened emotion. I recognized how my upbringing impacted on my way of hesitating before placing my own emotions at the centre of other people´s attention and how I was interacting in more subtle ways when my emotions were involved. I realized how paying attention to my patterns of behaviour in this quite unusual way of working together has contributed to my understanding of my research. I see how this enables me to work out conflict in less dramatic ways. However, I have also come to see the importance of giving a clearer account of myself and my own emotional response to others. Taking the idea of data as taken, constructed, and selected (Brinkmann, 2014:721) also means paying close attention to my own activities that create this research.

As a DMan student, reflection and reflexivity have become central to the methodological approach to my research in order to be able to detach myself enough to make plausible claims. Mowles distinguishes between reflection and reflexivity as two separate, yet connected, activities (2015:60).

> *"In reflecting we will be thinking and feeling deeply about something, possibly our own experience, whilst in becoming reflexive we are bringing that reflection back to ourselves and may be changed by it"* (ibid).

This understanding of reflexivity resonates with my methodological approach and has become a core approach during my research process. I understand reflexivity as a social process both emerging from my conversations with myself and through the reflexive collaboration with people with whom I work.

The final thesis consists of four projects and the current synopsis. Each project stands for itself and contributes with exploration and arguments related to the research theme. I began with an intellectual autobiography in project 1, reflecting on my practice and how I have become who I am as a practitioner. The three following projects consisted of analyses based on narratives about breakdowns as argued above. My research theme arises from the narratives and emerges through an iterative process of collaboration where insights from each project contribute to the further inquiry into the research theme in the next project. Each project is produced chronologically, starting with project 1 and put aside before starting the next project. The final synopsis takes another reflexive turn on my movement of thought and practice in the research. In this way, my movement of thought and practice will be demonstrated in the development of ideas from projects 1 to 4 and explicitly explained in the synopsis.

Each project in the thesis, and the synopsis, results from many iterations, and collaboration within this process is a central approach to my methodology, which will be described in the following.

## Collaborative and plural research

The collaborative approach that comes with being part of the DMan community is also taken up seriously in my thesis regarding what it means to contribute to knowledge and practice since this is a professional doctorate. The paradoxical perspective on the relationship between individual and social is methodologically played out in the thesis by emphasizing collaboration with others. Simultaneously, the writings are sole-authored by me, even if many people have influenced the ideas within them. However, even my interpretations and arguments are not to be understood as subjective since the subject is perceived as radically social, as argued above.

From a pragmatist perspective, there is no finding out how things in life really are, which means giving up on the positivist idea of gaining access to ultimate or absolute truth (Rorty, 1999:27). Instead, all key questions must be based on a combination of interpretation and justification regarding the hegemonic discourse through which it emerges (Stacey & Griffin, 2005:50), and understanding of some generality is then to take *"each instance of a phenomenon as an occurrence that evidences the operation of a set of cultural understandings currently available for use by cultural members"*

(Denzin, quoted by Brinkmann, 2014:723). This perspective can be related to my argument in P3, where I take a critical stand towards relativism and argue that truth is closely connected to experience in practice. In this way, my inquiry into breakdowns in my practice requires collaboration with others to seek understandings that resonate and are useful for others. The conversations in our learning sets and the wider DMan community are partly about this process.

Interpretation in my thesis is, as mentioned, based on reflexivity and inspired by Bourdieu and Wacquant, an ambition to *"translate highly abstract problems into thoroughly practical scientific operations, which presupposes … a very peculiar relation to what is ordinarily called theory and practice"* (1992:221). They argue for a researcher-position of radical doubt to develop scientific practice capable of questioning itself to know what it does (1992:236). In this way, reflexivity becomes, as mentioned above, a central part of my qualitative research since my arguments are not only based on the interpretations of theory and practice but also on a reflexive approach to the researcher's own way of thinking and the ongoing movement of thought.

Rorty argues for fellowship with the non-authoritarian and an ideological pluralism with the aim of justification to each other and relates to his concept of *fuzziness*, where he argues that it is plural fuzziness *"in the face of the unknowable, rather than certainty, which provides the impulse to dialogue and an ongoing search for meaning and understanding"* (Rorty, 1999:238). The idea of fuzziness resonates with the thinking of complex responsive processes in focusing on how human intentions are interwoven as a social process and new experiences and sense-making of the situation occur. As a result of this social process, research and knowledge could be understood from a perspective, whereby when knowledge is provided as a result of an individual (research) experience, then the legitimacy of the claims should be tested intersubjectively from a plural perspective in order to be plausible.

The collaborative and plural perspectives in my research are founded on an argument about the necessity of challenge in the way we think by engaging with standards outside of our own interests, concerns, and reflections in a community. This approach provides an opportunity to correct and revise our ideas (Pardales & Girod, 2006:302), which is at the heart of my scientific method.

My collaboration with the learning set and the wider DMan community has played a major role in engaging reflexively and challenging my own interpretations. However, to take the idea of pluralism seriously, I have found it important to broaden the collaborative processes and take my research findings up with my close colleagues and a community of researchers at the University College in Copenhagen. Furthermore, I have often shared my findings with the people involved in the breakdowns I inquire into to hear their perspectives. The aim of this has been to get diverse responses to my own interpretations in order to make sure that I did not collaborate in a chamber of echoes; encountering difference is a necessary part of this.

My research can be characterized as an iterative phronetic social science (Flyvbjerg, 2001) in terms of pragmatically governed interpretation of situations of breakdowns in my everyday experience. Simultaneously, in my research, I neither seek to uncover one inner meaning of practice nor is it the purpose to develop a determinative theory or universal methods (Flyvbjerg, 2001:140). As a phronetic social scientist, I draw on Rorty´s idea that political situations, which I find are an inherent part of organizational life, can be clarified by detailed stories about who is doing what to whom (1994:14) to explore entanglements and inquire into the topic of freedom. Then power becomes a central part of my inquiry to clarify the problems and risks we face in everyday organizational life and how we might find ways of engaging differently. According to Aristotle and Foucault, practice and freedom do not derive from theory. However, they both agree that *"Freedom 'is' a practice, not a result or a state of affairs. And phronesis is the intellectual virtue most relevant to the project of freedom"* (Flyvbjerg, 2001:128). I take this perspective to emphasize the need to justify my arguments, which in my research is a collaborative reflexive process with my colleagues at the DMan, different people I work with in my everyday practice, and my silent conversations with myself. For example, sharing my findings from my P4 with some of the managers from the municipality made me realize how they did not share my perceived need for speed in our process, which enabled me to research and write about this as well as subsequently to allocate more time to the dialogues between them. In this sense, I am approaching what Thomas refers to as exemplary knowledge (2010:578). My experience is suggested as being neither representative nor typical. However, with Thomas' words, *"it is interpretable only in the context of one's own experience - in the context in other words, of one's own phronesis"* (ibid).

Further, I also take in theories on the topics I inquire into, both those I agree and disagree with, to justify my own stand. The arguments are to be seen as the most persuasive account I can make at this point, which is not to say it would not be necessary to revise it in the light of new experience and understanding, but as the most plausible theory, for now.

## Collaborative autoethnography and narratives

To explore the situations of breakdowns in my practice, and with Rorty´s notion about paying attention to detailed stories with the ambition to clarify power structures and processes, I write narratives about such situations. These narratives are an alternative kind of data (compared to, e.g., interviewing). Writing them is a method by which we can inquire into the different intentions at stake in our everyday practice. The relevance of writing narratives as a foundation for research can be emphasized by the fundamental narrative structure of human life, which entails unpredictability (Czarniawski, 2004:13). Czarniawski argues how unpredictability does not imply inexplicability, but explanations become possible because of *"a certain teleology – a sense of purpose – in all lived narratives"* (Ibid). The sense of purpose resonates with the idea that good philosophical work should carry both arguments and vision. The philosopher's vision or intention is the great fact about him/her (Putnam, cited by Bernstein, 2016:26) and in my perspective, the researcher's intentions are to be considered in the process of doing research. Working with narratives relates to Brinkmann's concept of *creata* (2014:721), which refers to the idea of data being taken and creatively interpreted and not simply given. By paying attention to my visions as a researcher by giving an account of my own story and experiences and combining this with analysis of breakdowns in a cultural context, my research has many similarities with autoethnography as described by Lapadat (2017:589).

Ethnographic studies generally study cultural and conceptual phenomena, e.g., ideas, ways of thinking, symbols, meanings, and behavioural patterns (Alvesson & Sköldberg, 2018:108), while Carolyn Ellis describes autoethnography as an *"approach to research and writing that seeks to describe and systematically analyze (graphy) personal experience (auto) in order to understand cultural experience (ethno)"* (2011:273) and as a method that combines the characteristics of ethnography and autobiography (2011:275). The first project in my thesis can be seen as an autobiography, presenting an analysis of my individual story of work and how various experiences and influences have shaped me. The subsequent three projects include narratives about the above-described breakdowns in my recent personal experience of interacting with different people with whom I work. These narratives acknowledge my initial vision, my own motives, perspectives, emotions, and status (Lapadat, 2017:591), as well as the intentions of others.

The collaborative practice is significant for our way of working together at the DMan, which leads me to claim a collaborative autoethnographic approach for my research. However, this type of research is often described as multivoiced since more researchers work and write, tell, interrogate and analyze together (Lapadat, 2017:597), which is not the case in my research. I have systematically shared my thoughts and writings with my learning set and members of the wider DMan community and received their comments, questions, and responses. I have gained a degree of detachment from my own involvement and my perceptions of the intentions of others in my narratives. Based on the understanding that we are continuously making sense of the world through narratives, the idea of exploring these narratives – not only as a subjective process but as a collaborative process – is a core method in my research. However, the multivoiced character in my thesis is solely presented and authored by me and divides in this way from the collective writing presented by Lapadat.

Thus, the narratives I included are based on the experience of some sort of breakdown in my everyday practice. I chose to write about current situations where I was puzzled by interaction with others which raised animating questions relevant to my research. By writing several iterations of each project, my collaboration, especially with my learning set, led to the final decisions about what to include and exclude to explore themes that resonate with others. My conversations with the learning set and the wider DMan community helped me gain a more detached perspective on the situations in the narratives by contesting and questioning my understandings. Reading a wide range of literature had the same impact. The theories I considered are chosen because they seem to offer new perspectives that helped me make sense of my practice and provided understandings that were plausible explanations to other leaders in their practice.

Further, I have had two gatherings of groups of 20-25 colleagues at the University College of Copenhagen. I invited them to sit in a large circle while presenting my work so far and shared the questions by which I was still puzzled. Then I invited them in to comment one by one – both on my work but also to respond to the comments of others. They responded differently, but all shared that the themes of my research resonated with their experience, and they shared similar experiences of losing their sense of self and navigating the struggle for freedom. At the second meeting, which included a group of researchers from the University College, my methods were questioned. I did not start with a formal literature review which seemed incomprehensible for some and very inspiring to others. This conversation contributed to my efforts to explain my methodological approach more clearly and take a stand in doing research. My emphasis on how my research is problem-driven and not deriving from theory became more important to me through this conversation, and my endeavour to remain open was reinforced. I realized how my theme and my struggle for freedom also influenced my choice of methods. The multi-disciplinarity and the ongoing inquiry, as inspired by the DMan community, is an appropriate approach for me as it enables me to make sense of my practice based on abduction.

## Abductive reasoning

My research is based on abductive reasoning, which is a form of reasoning to be used when we want to understand situations of uncertainty (Brinkmann, 2012:46). The idea of abduction is understood as *"inference to the best explanation"* (Misak, 2004:16). This point raises a central question related to the legitimacy of knowledge, as mentioned above, and to generalizability.

Through induction, we observe or collect data and use it as the basis for formulating a theory. In contrast, deduction is about testing a theoretical hypothesis in order to validate or invalidate it. Conversely, abduction provides a different kind of generalization to both induction and deduction. Where induction argues for causal regularities, abduction provides a theory of understanding and not of explanation (Brinkmann & Tanggaard, 2015:457). The abductive reasoning is about understanding based on the best plausible explanations, for now, considering knowledge as always being incomplete (Bernstein, 1991:335-36). Unlike induction and deduction, both of which address the relationship between data and theory, abduction emphasizes the relationship between a situation and the inquiry (Brinkmann, 2014:722), which means that my research is problem-driven or driven by mystery, astonishment and "breakdown" and not driven by data or theory. This inquiry, therefore, begins with a puzzle and does not emerge from a traditional literature review but is a continual engagement with literature based on my experience of breakdowns in my practice. Rather than reaching definitions, I explore connections, relationships, and processes involved with the experience of freedom in the identity work of leaders.

The criteria for validity, reliability and generalizability within the social sciences have been widely discussed and several scholars argue how the generalization based on quantitative studies and rooted in the natural sciences is possible only to a limited extent, particularly by qualitative researchers within the social sciences (Thomas, 2012, Flyvbjerg, 2001). Alternative criteria have been proposed by qualitative researchers, where Bashir et. al. argues that *"validity in qualitative research means the extent to which the data is plausible, credible and trustworthy"* (2008:35) and others even argue how also in the natural sciences the concept of truth must be replaced with that of plausibility (Cellucci, 2014:530). The perception of plausibility is also central to Karl Weick and his perspective on sensemaking in organisations, in which he advocates that there is no need for accuracy, however it is necessary with *"something that preserves plausibility and coherence, something that is reasonable and memorable, something that embodies past experience and expectations, something that resonates with other people…"* (1995:60).  He further argues that *"plausible stories animate and gain their validity from subsequent activity"*. This perspective relates to my approach as a phronetical social scientist, as presented on page 137, researching plural meaning and understanding that helps me and others to move on in situations of breakdown. When the intention of my research is to empower others and myself, Finley argues that *"the researcher must explicitly address ethical and power dimensions – perhaps through a committed reflexive analysis"* (2006:326). Reflexivity is by Finley related to how the role of the researcher *"needs to be acknowledged and accounted for in the documentation of the research"* (2006:321), which resonates with my autoethnographic method, and the reflexive methodology as argued on page 136.

This premise indicates that the validity of the knowledge emerging from my research must be understood as plausible understandings of the phenomena into which I inquire. Plausibility in this regard means the degree to which the descriptions resonate with other people's experiences.

In this way, the degree of generalizability in my research must not be understood as truth but as a "good enough" understanding for now, which again opens for further interpretation (Mowles, 2011:82).  My arguments can be characterized as plausible understadings which find their validity insofar they have some resonance with the experience and/or imagination of others. The need for reflexivity as addressed by Finley demands according to both her and Alvesson & Sköldberg a certain capacity for dialogue within the research community and "the pluralism thus encouraged withiń individual research projects would then correspond to an increased pluralism at the level of the research community" (Alvesson & Sköldberg, 2018:375). Finley argues for five dimensions in evaluating outcomes in which the relation between the researcher and other participants are central and moves beyond a perspective on rigour and towards resonance and relevance (2006:322).. One of her criterias is communicative resonance, which also addresses the question of whether the findings draw people in and resonate with their own experience or alternatively disturb challenging unthinking complacency (ibid).   My engagement with the criteria of resonance has similarities with this perspective and is also inspired by Rosa´s argument that resonance includes dissonance (2019:184) which provides plurality to the plausible understandings and arguments I find. The degree of resonance has been continuously tested through dialogue with my fellow researchers at the DMan, with my colleagues at the University College, and with some of the people that appear in my narratives. The arguments are therefor based on a sensitive reflexive resonant collaboration with others and result in plausible understandings, that might help us move on I our practice.

The emerging character of the findings also means that the conclusions of this thesis are based on temporary insights that might be nuanced subsequently. Taking the approach of an autoethnographer, my own history, my points of view and ways of thinking will change over time, while the arguments of this thesis remain frozen in this written product (Lapadat, 2017:594). This idea that my arguments and my own way of thinking and understanding others is temporal, while the presentations of these in the form of this thesis are frozen, lead me to reflect on the ethics of my research and on how the presentation of moving understandings of self and others pose an ethical challenge to this kind of research.

## Ethics

Conducting autoethnographic research is considered in this thesis a highly ethical process of doing research that *"humanizes research processes and products and works to be more inclusive of how life is lived and how experience is storied"* (Adams et al., 2013: 673). However, this approach also raises ethical questions to be considered. Even though I argue against a split between subject and object in my inquiry into my own practice, there is a risk of losing the paradoxical relation between these two, which could lead to a rather narcissistic analysis. The collaboration with others, and especially with my learning set, has constantly challenged my understandings and thus reinforced the resonant character of my research by ensuring that I ask why my themes and questions might matter to other people. As mentioned above, it has been a constant endeavour to check the resonance of what I write with a wider community and avoid a situation where my research is self-indulgent and relies too strongly on my individual experience and sense-making.

In my understanding, the narratives about my work experiences are not wholly my own. They always implicate relational others (Lapadat, 2017:593). The narratives focus primarily on my own work experiences and the breakdowns in my practice, but the thickening of these narratives will inevitably involve the representation of other people. However, the focus of the narratives is not to analyze the people I work with in-depth as individuals but to explore the situations we are engaged in together and our interactions in these situations to find plausible understanding of our patterns of relating.

Even though I am writing about my own work-life experiences, a finger also points back to these identifiable others in my life, so how to portray these others constitutes another significant ethical challenge in this type of work, as suggested by Lapadat (2017: 593), which brings my attention to confidentiality and consent from the people who are portrayed in this thesis. When the people in my narratives are mentioned by name, I have changed their real names and anonymized the organisations within which they work. I have got consent from most of the people, who appear in the narratives, and the people I work with have been informed that I conduct research based on some of my everyday experiences in practice.

Even anonymized, some people can still be identified, which means that I might reveal situations where other people's reputation is at stake. In situations like these, I have asked for their consent and, in some instances, shared narratives and interpretations with them. This procedure is not to ensure that we agree but to thicken my narrative. In my P3, I included my own manager Grace, who can easily be identified despite the changed name. The fact that she was easy to identify and that the revealing of our relationship might impact on her subsequent relations to both me and others led to many considerations about how my way of representing her would affect us in the future. We have shared conversations about these issues, which led to her consent.

Ethical issues like these are frequently discussed and shared among the DMan research community members in general and in our learning set in particular. This point means paying attention to whom we include/exclude in the narratives, whether we represent others in ways they recognize, how we deal with possible disagreements about representation, and how to aspire to do no harm.

Lapadat addresses the ethical obligation towards others and emphasizes how researcher vulnerability is involved in autoethnographic research (2017: 594). In this thesis, I share highly revealing and formative stories about myself and my practice. The sequences of my history I chose to share are selected to inquire into patterns related to the research theme and not tell the whole story about me or my practice. However, presenting such stories publicly comes with the risk of judgment or stigma. I do not know how making the private visible will play out, as the written material takes a life of its own in the interpretation of others (ibid). The temporal aspect of the research reinforces this vulnerability since my way of thinking, and my professional practice will continue to move on after I finish this thesis. However, the arguments I have written are static and therefore not necessarily representative over time.

The ethical approach to my research, as it progressed, has been strongly inspired by John Dewey. He warned against reducing our moral obligations to something that can be handled with a specific set of rules or methods when he argues: "*a man's duty is never to obey certain rules; his duty is always to respond to the nature of the actual demands which he finds made upon him – demands which do not proceed from abstract rules nor from ideals, however awe-inspiring and exalted, but from the concrete relations to men and things in which he finds himself*" (1891:199-200). In this sense, the rules (e.g., made by university ethics committees) are not sufficient. Therefore, the collaborative practice of doing research has also involved ongoing conversations about making ethical judgments in the specific situations or relations in which I have found myself involved during this process. Writing about freedom can be equated with Foucault's ethics which is ethics antithetical to any type of *thought-police* (Flyvbjerg, 2001:127). Like Dewey, Foucault does not think that any kind of blueprint is generally useful, but according to Flyvbjerg refers to Aristotle's idea of phronesis, which relates to the sense of the ethically practical rather than a kind of science (Flyvbjerg, 2001:57). We thus cannot plan an ethical approach but must continuingly engage with ethical issues as they emerge in our practice. In this sense, the reflexive approach to my research, as described above, becomes a central part of meeting the ethical obligation involved in my research and making ongoing practical judgments in ethical matters.


## Limitations

After the ethical challenges of my research, the methodological approach, I have chosen, also comes with a set of limitations. The core idea in my research, following from the philosophies of pragmatism, is that our everyday life analyses are valid when they enable us and others to understand and act (Brinkmann, 2012:47). One could, however, argue that this approach comes with weak generalizability insofar that I am working with resonance to ensure that the research makes plausible claims and provides resonant understandings to others. Testing how my findings resonate with others brings richness to the presented narratives and the plausible understandings I present. However, even though I have engaged in collaboration with different groups of people to test the degree of resonance, I can only claim that the understandings are plausible explanations to a wider group of people across contexts but not necessarily generalizable to all.

Writing narratives is only one of several methods that can be used in ethnographically inspired research. My strong emphasis on this method can be seen as a limitation regarding the arguments I make. Different kinds of methods and the idea of triangulation can capture different aspects and make it possible to better determine a particular phenomenon (Alvesson & Sköldberg, 2018:109). The non-triangulation and the deselection of other techniques, e.g., various kinds of interviews, might have prevented a richer and more varied material.

With the endeavour to explore understandings of the complex responsive processes of human relating (Stacey & Mowles, 2016) involved in everyday organizational life, the plausible explanations I find do not provide a set of instruments or tools which can be applied. My way of conducting research, inquiring into the difficulties I experience in my work life takes the pragmatic perspective that analyses are valid when they enable us to understand or act (Brinkmann, 2012:47). However, in the arguments I make I do not prescribe actions for others, which might be perceived as a limitation by some.

To continue the process of critical heuristic reflexivity, I will present short summaries of each of the four research projects in the following sections. Further, I will take another reflexive turn on each project from my current standpoint to deepen and nuance my insights. This process also means bringing in new literature in order to continue this exploration.

## Project 1 – The contradiction of belonging and freedom

The reflexive autobiography that is my project 1 is about a search for belonging and freedom at the same time. I reflect on my upbringing with a strong cohesion in a large family circle, which was based on an ethos of always being helpful to each other. I learned that we should not put ourselves in the centre of people's attention as individuals, a cultural perspective influenced by what we call the *Law of Jante* in Denmark. This concept is not a real law but informal social norms described in an old novel.[1] The 'law' expresses that no individual should stand out from others, and you should not think you are something special or in any way better than others. Those commandments had a strong influence on our family at the time, and in hindsight, I see how this might have affected my interactions in life more than I thought before the reflexive process of doing this research.

In my P1, I came to think about my pattern of belonging to many different groups as a search for some degree of freedom from the social constraints that I found came along with belonging to a community. My wish to stand

---

[1] "En flygtning krydser sit spor" (A fugitive crosses his tracks) is a Norwegian novel written by Aksel Sandemose in 1933. The story is played out in a small Danish village and the Law of Jante is described for the first time in this book.

out as an individual, despite the constraining elements of, e.g., the *Law of Jante*, made me find ways of being on the edge of many different groups as a way to feel less disciplined, while at the same time not risking exclusion from the groups. One of the consequences of my belonging to various groups has been the experience of contradictions. I have become extremely skilled at navigating between several changing expectations, as I do not want to demean any of them.

Joining the staff at the University College, I got included in a group of social constructionist thinkers. The understanding of the world as consisting of many truths (Gergen & Gergen, 2004) resonated with my experience and my membership of many groups with different kinds of understandings, norms, and rules. However, at the same time, I found myself constantly questioning the certainties that come with the membership of a group, including the social constructionist approach to processes of forming the future and creating new identities through dialogue (e.g., Gergen & Gergen, 2004), which I have found unhelpful in situations where people felt stuck.

## Reflexive turn – a pattern of indeterminacy

Rereading my P1 brings my attention to a strong pattern of indeterminacy from the perspective of Honneth, which I also brought into my P3 (2000) and the way I tend to get lost in the perspectives of others. The *Law of Jante*, rejecting the legitimacy of treating oneself as the centre of attention, and my ways of navigating into various groups, have provided me with a well-developed sense of the different rules and values of others and the skill to engage with contradictions without bringing myself into the centre of potential conflicts. In hindsight, I see how I constantly negotiated my own identity in relation to the different groups and the rules and norms in these groups. The openness to others was a strong skill concerning different groups, but at the same time included a risk of not taking my own stand apart from being a person open to what Bernstein refers to as the otherness of others (1991:337). The elusive character that I became aware of in my P1 came with the consequence that I did not stand out as an individual in the way I wanted. At times, I found it difficult to relate to myself and found myself indecisive.

When Mead writes about values, he explores how people expressing their values inevitably provoke conflict and how it is an individual responsibility to express differences and formulate new standards of greater satisfaction than have existed so far (1934:387). He argues, at the same time, that all humans identify with their own interests and how we need to sacrifice our narrow self by developing a larger self that identifies with the interest of others (1934:386).

Now I see my pattern of being highly attentive towards the perspective of others has at times prevented me from paying attention to myself and expressing my own interests explicitly. Instead, I have found more subtle ways of bringing my values into the negotiations. What Mead refers to as the larger sense of self through identification with the interest of others must, in my view, be combined with Hegel´s perspective of "being with oneself in another" (Honneth, 2000:27) to stay in relation with both oneself and others. The paradoxical relation between individual and social, where we need to pay attention to both ourselves and others, emphasizes how the free experience of self is only possible when we know ourselves and voluntarily limit ourselves to recognize others (ibid:41). This is not an entirely deliberate process, but the degree of self-knowledge is partly implicit, based on our ongoing relationships with others. Relating openly to others must not come with the consequence of closing down the relation to self.

Freedom in my perspective comes with the strong sense of both self and others and the relationship between the two. My efforts to belong to many different communities enable me to engage with different norms and rules. If freedom is embracing the commitment to others, I need to investigate my freedom to act into these. So, do I want to give up the ability to adapt that comes along with belonging to many groups and then accept the consequences, e.g., the risk of losing my sense of self or feeling invisible? I see now how I can still negotiate various roles in very different assignments at the University College and how my collaboration within every assignment must consider both my interests and the interests of others. Sometimes this might entail that I withdraw from a task or am excluded if we cannot find ways of moving on together, which is a risk I want to take. Being with oneself in another is not about either/or, but how I sometimes adapt to the views of others and they to mine and in other situations to a lesser degree or maybe there is no adaptation at all.

This mutual commitment to both self and others includes an ethical responsibility to participate in the ongoing conversations and formations of present relationships in a group. The moral judgment that Mead (1934:387) points out should be viewed in the light of a social situation} in which both I and others take part. Taking an ethical responsibility for the development of a community, or in my working practice and organizational situation, comes with an obligation to participate as an individual with others. One could argue that we can never not participate. However, participation from the paradoxical perspective means acknowledging our responsibility for both self and others in our ways of relating and interacting with others. The mutual responsibility and interdependence between individuals in these processes are highlighted in Bernstein's interpretations about plurality and democracy. He states:

> *"…plurality does not mean that we are limited to being separate individuals with irreducible subjective interests. Rather it means that we seek to discover some common ground to reconcile differences through debate, conversation, and dialogue"* (1983:223).

From the perspective of my professional role as a temporary leader, as presented in P2, I have been aware of the impossibility of taking a neutral position in the processes in which I am involved. I found it important to address the emerging conflict, and by paying attention to this issue, I took a stand. During this research process, I have found myself increasingly comfortable bringing my own opinions or values into the processes in which I work – not as truths from the expert, but as my experience and perspectives that might or might not resonate with others.

At the same time, I have the *Law of Jante* in the back of my head, telling me to constantly be doubtful about how much any process should be about me. Mead´s point about moral judgment helps me to see this as an ongoing process in each situation within which I work. The negotiations about finding time and space for both me and others became central to not losing either perspective and taking part in the joint responsibility for the present community with whom I work. Being both formed by and simultaneously forming the groups you belong to addresses a shared responsibility in which every individual contributes. Indeterminacy or the idea of neutrality might, in this way, come from a lack of attention and responsibility for the ongoing forming of which every participant is part. I see now how refusing to accept the role as an expert does not, as imagined, necessarily make me lose freedom but enables me to interact with my own sense of self. This refusal does not prevent me from simultaneously taking the position of either doubt or openness to others. I see now how giving a strong account of myself by sharing my own beliefs and emotions can enable the people I work with to gain a sense of who they are and have an ongoing conversation about how we can move on together.

At the end of P1, I was puzzled by my experiences of feeling stuck in situations at work where, in some of my assignments, we could not form the future as we wished to. I was particularly interested in the relation between being and becoming to find new ways of developing others in a specific direction and held onto the perspective of being a consultant or teacher who could control processes, even though I rejected the idea of thinking of myself like that. The paradoxical relation between our own historically formed identity (being) and the possibilities for the future development of identities (becoming) indicates how we are both enabled and constrained by our own history.

My reflections in my P1 led me to explore the relations between the individual and the social and the contradictions that emerge in our inter-relational practice. The process of writing my P1 was difficult and took longer than I expected compared to some other students. I made sense of this experience with my learning set because writing in my second language, while having a busy schedule at work, had slowed me down. Looking back, I see how unfamiliar it felt to write so much about myself and how I found it difficult to prioritize this process as it was all about me. Not speaking much in the larger community was also raised as a reason for the slower pace. In hindsight, I see a pattern in all my projects, in which it is difficult for me to stick to one theme and close an argument down, which relates to my theme of remaining open as a way to experience freedom.

My learning set helped me realize how my background in a working-class family and the *Law of Jante* might have made me ambitious to prove my intellectual skills by having high professional standards, but at the same time not believing that my capacity was something special or good enough. My autobiography contributed, in this sense, with insights about my own historically formed identity and how I myself and my research were both enabled and constrained by this process. Reflections like these have made me feel a stronger sense of freedom to improvise into alternative ways of engaging with my own patterns in my interplay with others. I perceived a way to freedom combined with not belonging too strongly to any group and sought independence in this way. By accepting how we are always interdependent, my sense of freedom changed.

My awareness of my openness towards plurality emerged from my autobiography and has inspired my research on identity and freedom. However, my research has also come to involve exploring several other themes as steps on the way for me to make plausible claims about the complexity in the field of my research. The willingness to explore my ideas from multiple perspectives can be considered as an impetus to learning while at the same time as avoidance of taking a specific stand.


## Project 2 – Power relations and identity

My project 2 narrative is about my experience of having contradictory thoughts and emotions after a one-day leadership development seminar with a group of managers and their support staff in the Danish welfare sector. The purpose of the day was to initiate the development of their leadership practice in response to recent changes in politics, economy, and strategy. I was asked to facilitate processes during the one-day seminar to support this development. At preliminary meetings with the planning group, we had prepared a detailed agenda for the day, which revealed their need to control to an unusual extent.

At the beginning of the day, the managers presented their visions for the future. Inspired by our conversations at the preparatory meeting and descriptions of many reactions of frustration because of huge budget cuts, I gave a short presentation about complexity and emotions in organizational change. As a result, a conflict between the managers and the support staff broke out. The tone became extremely hostile, and an HR consultant almost burst into tears. My response to the conflict was to reflect on what was going on, which meant that the conflict was more clearly articulated and strong emotions were expressed. After completing the day, it became obvious to me that the planning team felt very uncomfortable with the level of conflict and that the manager did not know what to do.

The experience was one of contradictory feelings. First, I was afraid that they did not think I had done my job well enough. I feared that they would blame me for letting the conflict increase and, as a consultant not being able to run a constructive process for them. I was puzzled by my own role as to how I had contributed to this conflict. At the same time, I felt content for having stayed with the conflict and not having escaped immediately by drawing attention to the future they wished to create instead. I wondered why I responded to the process with such mixed emotions, which I felt as pressures and pulls on my identity.

Reflecting on the narrative, I saw that I was responding to different contradictory ways of thinking about learning at the same time. By inquiring into various understandings of learning in my P2, I realized that I was trying to meet expectations from various perspectives. The social constructionist inspiration made me facilitate a process where the participants already began to form the future through dialogue (Gergen & Gergen, 2005). I see now how thinking about a future process almost prevented us from engaging with the present and what we were doing together. In contrast, my inspiration from the DMan community inclined me towards insisting on reflection about what was going on when the conflict was articulated. As described by Brinkman, Dewey's perspective on learning emphasizes how our actions should be in focus, that we should relate to our concrete experience and that reflection on our breakdowns is seen as an essential element in our efforts to learn (Brinkmann, 2013:164). I see that I was disciplined by my earlier close connection with the social constructionist community. When staying with the conflict, instead of turning the situation into wishes for the future, I may have disrupted the understandings and expectations of a consultant. The fact that the conflict arose and that I stayed with it and did not "make" it go away provoked anxiety in both me and the participants as it was different from our more well-known practice, based on forming futures.


Reflexive turn – interdependency between individual and social
My exploration of power relations and power struggles in project 2 has influenced my further understanding and my subsequent practice. Understanding my everyday practice as negotiations of identity in power relations has made me realize that my practice always entails political judgments about how to find ways to engage with others and express my stand. Acknowledging power relations as an inevitable part of organizational life, and my self-inquiry into the consequences of obeying the *Law of Jante*, has also made me less anxious about entering into conflicts. At the one-day

seminar, I found the freedom and courage to hold on to the conflict that arose and to be myself with the others. This process enabled the participants to discuss the power struggles between them even though this evoked unpleasant emotions. I find that I invite the people I work with more often to talk more openly about conflicting positions. I even find myself challenging truisms by presenting opposite and counter-arguments to challenge dogmatic understandings. Paying attention to the power relations emphasizes the idea of inviting others to engage with difference and the ambiguities involved in organizational life. I can invite others to talk more openly about conflict by not avoiding potential conflict myself. However, doing this in a deterministic way, by insisting to talk about conflict might be considered as a violent act and end up in alienation if we do not pay attention to what is going on for others. The response I got from the participants in the P2 narrative was that they felt extremely uncomfortable talking about their conflicts, and the anxiety this provoked needed to be dealt with afterwards.

In P2, I touched on a definition of my own practice. In continuation of my pattern of indeterminacy, I did not have a quick or clear answer when my learning set colleagues asked me whether I am a consultant, teacher, or facilitator. Inspired by Mowles' (2009) argument about how consultancy can be considered a position of temporary leadership, I see how I have been trying to understand my own role as similar to those with whom I often work. In project 4, I write about being a co-participant while remaining different from other participants simultaneously. Every participant may have different associations with the group in which they engage. As leaders, they also take the role of being both included and at the same time not equally included in a group. This point emphasizes Mowles' argument and makes me understand my own practice as a temporary leader and as an equal and unequal participant. Thinking about leadership as non-heroic, since no individual can control what is played out in groups, does not mean that people in groups are equal. The power relations are part of the rhythms we must pay close attention to improvise into the present, and equality and inequality can be played out. In the experiences I later explain in P4, I felt how the formal space with the microphones and the photos of former mayors on the wall affected our interactions and how I felt the responsibility for the process was being located with me and how this made me unable to engage in the conversations as an equal participant.

After rereading my project 2, I realize that writing about identities and power from both a Foucauldian and an Eliasian perspective draws on two seemingly different traditions within the studies of identity in organisations. In a review article, Andrew Brown advocates how the theme of identity can be approached from discursive, dramaturgical, symbolic, socio-cognitive, and psychodynamic perspectives (2017 & 2019) but argues that identity is closely related to agency and how a range of work assumes how individuals have considerable agency in identity matters, while others take identity to be the effect of power relations (Brown, 2019:14). From the perspective of Elias, I see how identities are both being formed by and also playing a part in forming the power relationships of which they become part. This claim is supported by Mead when he argues for the interconnection between self – reconstruction and social reconstruction:

> *Thus the relations between social reconstruction and self or personality reconstruction are reciprocal and internal or organic; social reconstruction by the individual members of any organized human society entails self or personality reconstruction in some degree or other by each of the individuals, and vice versa, for since their selves or personalities*

> *are constituted by their organized social relations to one another, they cannot reconstruct those selves or personalities without also reconstructing, to some extent the given social order, which is, of course, likewise constituted by their organized social relations to one another* (1934:309).

Within this quote, Mead draws attention to the interdependency between the individual and social in identity processes, which I take to mean that the self-reconstruction, or the ongoing processes of forming identity, constitute our patterns of social relating while at the same time, vice versa, the social reconstruction constitutes individual identities. Identities must as such be understood as a radically social phenomenon. In my research, this understanding of identity does not reduce the individual to only being formed by the social and through that disregard the idea of individual agency. Exploring power relations at the one-day seminar in my P2 narrative is, therefore, not enough. My understandings of these must reflexively be brought back to myself to find new ways of engaging in these kinds of power *games.* The ongoing reflection about what is going on for me and others in the situations I inquire into makes me see how leadership has similarities to research practice and how the leader as an individual carries a responsibility. Inquiring into what is going on in everyday work life leaves us with an ethical obligation to find our ways of moving on together with both our own interests and the interest of others is considered. This situation calls for ongoing practical judgments about our own actions.

In his review article, Brown argues how some key questions about identity remain to be answered and emphasizes that the connection between macro performances of groups or organisations and how they are connected to the micro identity processes of the participants or employees is still a mystery (2019:17). With Elias´ ideas of we- and I-identity from my P2, and Mead's arguments about how individuals and societies paradoxically form and are formed by each other, it might bring light to the connection between the micro and macro levels suggested by Brown. My dialectic approach to individual and social leads to my perspective on identity, where Mead supplements my explorations in project 2 based on Foucault and Elias. The I/Me dialectic I explore in my project 3 leads to understanding identity as an ongoing dialectical process based on social constraint and individual agency, which makes identities temporal and incomplete. Losing the paradoxical character of these self-organising processes might lead us to alienation from either self or others by not acknowledging the interdependence between the individual and their social worlds. Like Mead and Elias, I do not understand structure and agency as macro and micro levels but as two phases of the same social process.


## Project 3 – Sense of self and others - visibility and invisibility

My P3 narrative revolves around the theme of belonging and freedom through a specific example of not prioritizing and still not allowing others to help me reduce my number of assignments. My breakdown in the narrative was about not wanting to give up any of my responsibilities and about the experience of feeling invisible. My puzzle was about why, despite a heavy workload, I ended up accepting another assignment once again.

The narrative took place when the University College had just merged with another big University College in Copenhagen. Because of a heavy workload, which left me dissatisfied with my efforts, I invited my manager, Grace, to discuss my assignments and how they should be reprioritized.

In our conversation, she told me to stop my planned teaching on our leadership education. A knot tightened in my stomach, and I started to explain why this was not a good decision. She interrupted and said that no matter what she would suggest, I would have perfectly good arguments as to why this was not an option. I was emotionally affected by her decision and felt a strong urge to resist. Subsequently, I did not withdraw from my teaching commitments but negotiated that I should not teach quite as much as planned. I told Grace about my decision, which she accepted.

Shortly afterwards, I had a feeling of being invisible. I was rarely invited into new assignments or asked to contribute and did not attend the same number of meetings as before. I felt that the new managers from the merged University College did not know of my level of experience and competence, and I heard them talking as if they did not know about my field of work.

Project 3 once again emphasizes the importance of not losing the sense of the paradoxes in life and not being tempted to adopt idealized understandings to escape from ambiguity and contradictory conditions for organizational life. Merleau-Ponty´s perspective on chiasms, where he reinforces the existence of two different sides of a phenomenon (Helin et al., 2014: 418), helped me see how I was idealizing the idea of visibility in my organization and thought the only way to reach it was by working harder and in that way staying part of many groups. I realized that invisibility might be a good thing at times and need not lead to a lack of recognition. Visibility is about being visible in relation to specific others and being visible to yourself. I see how my need for recognition was rewarded by receiving a little recognition from many groups. However, I was not aware that being on the edge of many groups might come with a lesser visibility and weaker recognition. My experience was that the recognition did not aggregate, and such fragmentation did not feel like recognition in the public realm. No strong belonging to any group, as teacher, facilitator, internal consultant, or researcher, might have made me an inferior member of the various groups and, therefore, not clearly visible.

Losing the understanding of the paradoxes might result in a tendency to respond with either dogmatism or relativism and prevent us from learning more and taking a stand but allows us to both take a position while remaining open to renegotiate or hold on to our stand in relation to others. I see how my endeavour to belong to many groups prevented me from critically engaging with the question as to which groups I most wanted to belong to and from which to receive recognition. I was not ready to stop teaching, unable to withdraw from ongoing consultancy commitments, resisted excluding myself from the collegial meetings, while still holding on to my wish to write my doctoral thesis. My identity felt at stake and dependent on my belonging to all of the groups. Subsequently, I see how I have now allowed myself to stop teaching and withdraw from internal development groups to take my identity as a researcher more seriously.

This project also illustrates that even seemingly simple everyday considerations can imply pressures and pulls on our identity and emphasizes the need for ongoing hyper reflection (Merleau-Ponty, 1968:33), focusing our bodily involvement in the world or reflexivity, which from Mead's perspective, is closely connected to becoming a self. Both perspectives argue for taking oneself as an object to oneself, and in combination, they emphasize both body and mind in self-reflexive processes. To me, it also underlines the importance of paying attention to both past, present, and intentions for the future in the continuing processes of negotiating identity. In this way, freedom is closely and paradoxically connected to constraints, and freedom might only be achieved by accepting that we are both enabled and constrained at the same time and by finding ways of recognizing or compromising both our own and others' needs and demands. So, my wish to belong enabled me to adapt to many groups and take on multiple assignments. Simultaneously, it constrained my sense of my professional identity and my freedom to say no to potential assignments.

## Reflexive turn – being with oneself in another

In writing my P3, it became clear to me how the paradox between determinacy – indeterminacy has played a significant part in making sense of my own history and ongoing way of engaging with the world. I was determined to stay open to the otherness of others, and in these efforts, I lost my sense of self and was, e.g., unable to take my experience of too much work seriously. Realizing how this pattern emerged and was played out in my work life, I felt both shame and a determination to change it. I do not wish to be evasive in my ways of engaging with what is going on, and even though I still feel like a slave of old habits, I see the importance of becoming more visible concerning myself and others. In the narrative, I reached out for help, but Grace´s inability to be helpful might have resulted from my determined indeterminacy. So, in order for other people to relate to me, I must be more visible and break my pattern of not placing myself at the centre of attention. It is easier for me to say no today, and it does not come with the same discomfort that it did earlier. However, as mentioned above, forming identities are not only individually held processes. It has been my experience that we are socially both enabled and constrained in our relation to ourselves.

In my project 4, I elaborate on the suffering from indeterminacy I described in P3, and write about being determinately indeterminate, which to me means that I can hold on to the curiosity and openness towards others while not losing the sense of myself in the process. Relating in a radically open way to others is and can still be part of my identity. However, the Hegelian concept of *being with oneself in another* (Honneth, 2000) to me means never neglecting my sense of self. Becoming aware of my pattern of indeterminacy and sharing this with others might enable me to more freely find new ways of interacting with others and enable my co-workers to relate differently to me.

Reflexivity and the antidogmatic approach to the ambiguities in my everyday relations to others have become cornerstones in my practice. The memberships of many different groups and thought collectives have enabled me to see situations from many different perspectives and relate to different people and come with the possibility for an enlarged sense of self if I am able, in Mead's terms, to come back to myself from the outside (1936:88). If not brought back to oneself, there is a risk of relativism. This process does not entail finding ways of getting things right with myself and others in my everyday work life. Instead, it means turning my attention to coping with the contingencies of human life and gaining a new sense of community (Bernstein, 1983:203). Exploring the idea of visibility and invisibility in this narrative made me reflect on my idealisations of visibility and ask myself why it feels more or less important to be visible.

I think that allowing myself to focus on my own work-life experience as an employee led to an embodied understanding of the above-mentioned ambiguities of organizational life that I had experienced earlier on. I found it embarrassing that I was unable to say no to assignments while at the same time asking Grace to help me reduce my workload, and I found it puzzling how difficult change in identities can be. Rosa, whom I draw on in my P4, writes about how desires and fear are often intermixed and how the increasing demand to adapt to stay connected to the world is connected with the fear of rejection (2019:118). However, the accelerated speed and the pace with which we are expected to adapt comes with a risk of alienation from both self and others and, according to Rosa, psychological crises such as burnout as a result (2019:2).

Hegel´s understanding of dialectic combined with Merleau-Ponty´s development of this in his idea of chiasms, where thesis and antithesis do not necessarily join into synthesis, but opposites and ambiguity should be accepted, led to a reconciliation for me with the understanding that contradictions exist in both paradoxical and chiasmic ways. My unwillingness to belong too strongly to one group, and a specific set of understandings, norms, and rules, have taught me that idealisations tend to avoid plurality, which I believe to be a core aspect of human and organisational life. I also became aware of how the emergence of identities is not only about consciousness and the ability to dream about what the future should be. No matter how much I wanted, and still seek to, reduce my workload, this is an ongoing challenge for me since my powerful pattern is hard to break. Change in identity is hard to facilitate in others and is also not only something we easily decide for ourselves.

From my arguments in my P3 about the human capacity of taking yourself as an object to yourself and considering your inevitable visibility as a person, individual agency comes through noticing the emergence of identity and finding ways of engaging with it. I see how I am under pressure to perform at the University College in order to make a profit and how what Rosa refers to as the constraints of competition and optimization (2019:236) continue to lead me to be a good employee who can take on various assignments and put in many hours. Rosa argues how our efforts in meeting demands leave us with no time to rest or enjoy success. He points out that we perceive signals of recognition from our superiors as purely strategic (ibid), which resonates with my experience with Grace. Once, one of my colleagues told me that it was hard for her that Grace always measured her performance up against mine, which brings me to understand how I have not only been adapting to the idea of competition and optimization at the University College - I have also reinforced it. Such insight leaves me with a different kind of sensemaking and a stronger ambition to break this pattern. I both want to be a good employer and a good colleague, and not overwork with the contradictions this might entail.

## Project 4 – Standing firm with fragile feet on volatile ground

In my fourth project, my inquiry is based on a narrative from an ongoing assignment with a continuingly enlarged group of managers in a Danish municipality. I address the experience of how ways of relating to both self and others, as suggested by Mead, are temporally shifting. In this assignment, the first task was to give two presentations of my view on collaboration and the ambiguities and conflict this might evoke and then invite the participants to reflect on their task to collaborate closely with each other to coordinate their different efforts regarding young citizens with social problems. Both the first presentation and the following discussion resulted in shared reflections and conversations where the leaders appeared both open and curious towards each other. As they wanted to continue the work, I was asked to describe a one-year leadership development process for this group and more of their colleagues. Our agreement about a programme was based on a reflexive approach to their everyday practice to continue exploring their efforts to work closely together as a collaborative community of leaders. We arranged a range of new meetings, including an enlarged group of leaders.

My experience in the first meeting in this larger group was that even though I had a strong sense of how I was able to engage with the group, based on my previous interactions with several of the managers and on the reflexive process I had suggested, things did not turn out in any way I had imagined. My earlier understanding of my temporary leadership within this group became disrupted when I found that they did not continue the reflexive conversations after a few new participants had joined the group. Since this had now been formulated as the purpose of the programme, I was frustrated by the conversations that pointed to instrumental solutions, such as needing an information system, and I found myself fighting to resist what I perceived as some of the participants' assumptions that what went on at the meeting was my responsibility.

My initial worries that working reflexively would lead to no change in their everyday collaboration turned into the frustration that we could not even work reflexively, which I realized had now become a goal in itself. At this first meeting, I felt like an outsider and found it difficult to relate to the participants in the ongoing conversations. Even though I still held on to some of my understandings of my role as a consultant, i.e., not being in control of what went on, I found myself standing on volatile ground experiencing awkwardness in relating to some of them and not listening closely.

Reflexive turn – emergent rhythms and resonance
Paying attention to the temporalities and the changing rhythms in my ongoing work with the group of managers has been highly influential in thinking about freedom and leadership. The idea of taking our own experience seriously is a core method in the DMan community. In my

project 4 it became clear to me how this is required to experience freedom as the freedom to engage with whatever emerges in our everyday work life. I relate the degree of freedom we experience to the sense of agency we can find in our ongoing interactions. The emergent character of what rhythms we are to engage in requires us to explore these to find possible ways of responding and moving on together. If we abstract from these everyday experiences in an effort to evade difficult emotional reactions, differences, and conflicts, we cannot experience freedom within this interdependence. The experience of the changing rhythms in my interactions with more or less the same group of leaders makes me realize how we must stay open for whatever emerges in the present or with the words of Lefebvre: *"There is no identical absolute repetition. … Not only does repetition not exclude difference, it also gives birth to them; it produces them"* (2019:16-17). In the encounter I present in the narrative, I was caught by surprise but found myself unable to inquire into the present to find ways of improvising in finding ways of *being myself with others*. From this perspective, my experience of being unable to engage reflexively with the group of managers helped me find new ways in our ongoing work. It did not work on the day of the meeting. However, through my collaborative dialogues about what emerged, we could find new locations and allocate more time to group dialogues in the following meetings.

Looking back, the experience of writing my P4 has made me relate leadership to research. Gaining a sense of freedom in the emergence of leadership requires an ongoing inquiry into the present rhythms and power relations in which we are entangled. I see how I tend to rush over some of these processes, trying to escape from the contradictions and ambiguities involved in these processes. In the narrative, I found how I was caught up in my desire to engage reflexively with this group as we had earlier on. Instead of staying with this emotion and exploring how I was puzzled by our interaction, I got irritated and felt inadequate. The lack of attention towards these processes and the acceleration in our interactions with each other comes with the risk of alienation from both ourselves and others. When we perceive freedom not as liberation from interdependencies but as the freedom to engage with the fact that selves emerge within a complex pattern of interactions with others, freedom comes with the ongoing exploration of these interdependencies. The idea that freedom is about individual agency, whereas constraint is about social structures, collapses in this perspective. By not belonging too strongly to any group but maintaining my membership of various groups, I have sought a sense of freedom from one group's specific norms and values. From this perspective, this only led to a different kind of interdependence in which my pattern of indeterminacy emerged.

In this way, leaders need to engage in everyday research into their present work-life and improvise into rhythms and power relations that inevitably contain complexity and uncertainty. Resonant relationships then become central for the experience of freedom to develop agency based on the exploration of mutual interdependency. However, the desire for resonant relationships might in itself become a constraint for experiencing resonance. Rosa argues how *"every desire is at bottom a desire for resonance (and every fear a fear of resonance´s loss) the ideal resonant experience is itself free from desire, insofar as desire always means striving for change, to transform and overcome one´s present state or situation, while a resonant experience carries its fulfillment in itself"* (2019:120). The desires or intentions with which we interact in everyday work life might, in this sense, constrain our relationship with both self and others. This approach emphasizes the importance of paying attention to how these affect our relationships and accepting the uncontrollability of how our interactions are played out. In thinking further about Rosa's idea of resonance, I draw on his perspective of how resonance can neither be found in pure harmony nor imply the absence of alienation. I claim that only by becoming reflexive about our experiences of harmony, conflict, and alienation can we recognize both ourselves and others. I needed the perspective of others in reflecting on what went on in that meeting in the large group in my P4. By listening to how the managers wished for more time to talk, I found that I was caught up with an increase in pace, even though this was not what I wanted.

Inquiring into the P4 narrative has enabled me to move on in my relationship with the group of leaders in this specific Danish municipality in new ways. I now understand this as ongoing negotiations of my leadership practice with a careful exploration of what is emerging in our interactions with each other and how I can find ways of engaging with my interest and the interests of others in mind. Also, I understand how I need to pay attention to the cultural idealisations that appear, e.g., the wish for speed and specific goals of the processes in which we engage. I see in the narrative how I continue to get caught up in these powerful patterns, such as rushing towards a conclusion and enabling predetermined goals. However, instead of trying to escape from them, I realise how freedom can arise from taking these experiences seriously by sharing these in conversations with others and using these insights to find new ways of moving on together. The continued conversation with the leaders from my P4 narrative, in which we have shared such reflections, has, in my opinion, helped us in our process. Accepting that I cannot control or predict outcomes has enabled me to be more present with myself and others. The argument I make here is how the understanding of freedom *to* enables us to repair and staying in relation with others, whereas the perspective of freedom *from* means a break in relations and lack of resonance. Further, the idea of staying in relations will, in this perspective, enable a higher degree of freedom, as we can negotiate who we are in relation to others.

The fact that I have shared my insights from my P4 with the participants from the municipality has, in hindsight, been an unusual way of putting myself more in the centre of the process. One day the project manager of the programme asked me what we should do when I no longer had my insights from this research process to bring in, which made me realize the value of research as an integrated part of everyday leadership.

Based on the findings in my projects and the elaborations of this synoptically reflexive turn on the four projects, I will turn to unfold the main arguments concerning the negotiation of identities and the struggle for freedom and individual agency in everyday collaborative leadership evolving from these processes.

## Key arguments

Having reflected further on my projects and thought about the connections between them, I propose three main arguments:

1. **The process of negotiating identity in the emergence of leadership practice involves disruptions, ambiguities, and contradictions.**

2. **Paradoxically, there is a greater potential for freedom within the emergence of leadership with the acceptance and exploration of interdependencies. In doing so, we**

**more fully recognize ourselves and others through resonant relationships.**

3. **Leaders need to pay attention to their engagement with recurrent idealisations, i.e. the contemporary pressure for speed in organizational life, which might contribute to the illusion of freedom through individual agency.**

In the following, I will unfold, elaborate, and substantiate the three main arguments regarding my research theme:

*An inquiry into the paradoxical and contradictory experience of freedom and constraint within the social process of negotiating leadership identity.*

## Argument 1: The process of negotiating identity in the emergence of leadership practice involves disruptions, ambiguities, and contradictions

The theme of identity has become a major theme within management and organisational studies in recent years (Brown, 2019:7, Winkler, 2018:120). The anti-essentialist perspective on identities as a process rather than a product (Alvesson, Loacker & Sandberg, 2013) and as fluid and constituted by discourse, has according to Alvesson et al. almost become a hegemonic discourse itself (2009:5). Processes of the never-finished formation of identities have been widely explored using the notion of identity work addressing activities that individuals engage in to support and construct their understanding of self (Brown, 2019:9). In studies of these processes, a common debate focuses on whether identities or identification can be chosen by autonomous individuals (Gergen, 1991) or mainly ascribed to historical and structural forces (Foucault, 1982).

In a literature review, Brown (2017:308) highlights how several scholars address how identities are neither simply chosen nor merely allocated, and Knights & Clarke (2014) argue for a dialectical approach to structure and agency by considering organizational identification and the emergence of identity as pragmatic, generally social and emotionally charged.

In contrast to these more commonly expressed process perspectives, I argue that identities emerge in a paradoxical relation between radically social selves. I emphasize that identities are neither individually taken nor given by the organizational environment but emerge in present interweaving processes of interdependency between thoroughly social selves. However, my argument is close to the dialectic perspective, highlighting the paradoxical relation where self and others are mutually constituting.

I draw on the work of Norbert Elias, who advocates how individuals are simultaneously formed by and forming the social. He states:

*"One finds then – in adopting a wider, dynamic viewpoint instead of a static one – that the vision of an irreducible wall between one human being and all others, between inner and outer worlds, evaporates to be replaced by a vision of an incessant and irreducible intertwining of individual beings, in which everything that gives their animal substance the quality of a human being, primarily their psychical self-control, their individual character, takes on specific shape in and through relationships to others."* (1991:32)

He emphasizes the importance of understanding to which groups we belong and states how *"each ´I´ is irrevocably embedded in a ´we´"* (1991:62) where, in my experience, my endeavour to belong to many groups emphasizes what Mead terms as *"the capacity of being several things at once"* (1934:73). In his understanding of the self, Mead draws on his understanding of the I – me dialectic, as described in my P3. His paradoxical understanding between the self and the social involves the adaptation of the I. However, it is an adaptation that affects not only the self but also the social environment, which helps to constitute the self (1934:214). Further, he argues that what needs to be recognized is *"that the character of the organism is a determinant of its environment"* (1934:215). In this perspective, individual agency and social structures must be considered mutually constituted. Therefore, identity cannot be perceived based on the individual and the social conceived as being at different levels of social reality.

This point suggests a temporal approach to the ongoing identity work in which humans are engaged. Our membership of different groups with different rules and norms, which provides us with an experience of anticipating the reactions of others, is brought with us into our present lives. However, there is no guarantee that our anticipation of the response from others is correct when human identities are continuously affecting and affected by the environment. In my P4, even when interacting with the same group of leaders, I found myself enabled and constrained in very different ways from the first meeting to the second. When identities emerge, and leadership is practised, it affects the group that again pushes back and enables identity in new ways. When I proudly engaged with the conflict that arose in my P2, the anxiety this provoked in the group also changed my confidence about my own choices and constrained my sense of doing the right thing.

My membership in various groups provides me with the capacity to be different based on my different interactions within these groups. However, due to our membership in groups, we draw on our past experiences and are simultaneously constrained by these. As illustrated in my P2, my shared history of forming positive futures with the group of managers made it difficult, confusing, and emotionally painful to stay with the conflict that arose in the group. This endeavour had become important and possible for me, e.g., due to my membership in the DMan community. This case emphasizes the contradictory character of identity negotiations in our everyday work life because of being formed by and forming various kinds of groups. Our different interactions and negotiation of selves in one group might collide with our identity in another group. Simultaneously, the temporality in the paradoxical relations to groups also might come with ambiguous and contradictory norms and rules compared to earlier.

Based on my research, I argue that historically and culturally formed identities play a significant part in the making of our present selves. My belonging to the group of social constructionist thinkers and my family background, based on the *Law of Jante*, are examples of power relations in the ongoing formation of my professional identity. The idea of the world consisting of many truths (Gergen & Gergen, 2004), and the perception that one should not think too highly about oneself, made me in both my P2 and P3, try to recognize the perspective of various others to the degree that made me indeterminate and unable to prioritize and take a stand. As individuals, we come with a specific history. We are entangled in strongly embodied habitual ways of thinking, feeling, and interacting, which form our intentions for the future and our ways of interacting with the present. In this sense, all humans are continuously (re)formed, often in contradictory ways. The sense of self must be undertaken through ongoing exploration since it emerges in different groups and at different times in our everyday practice.

I claim how the capacity to be several things comes with a risk of relativism and indeterminacy (for further explanation, see my P3) to not judge but to live up to different expectations and maintain our membership of various groups. This point relates to the consequence of losing the paradoxical perspective on individual and social. My argument of a paradoxical understanding of identity relies on acknowledging interdependency and the need for mutual recognition between humans (Honneth & Margalit, 2001). With inspiration from Hegel´s concept of *"being with oneself in another"* (Honneth, 2000), I argue how there is a risk of getting lost in either ourselves or in the other if we do not take the idea of interdependency seriously. In my experience, I became aware of my history with the Danish cultural *Law of Jante* and a pattern of indeterminacy, resulting from a weak sense of agency, e.g., unable to reduce my number of assignments and let any of the people I worked with down. Getting lost in oneself is, according to Honneth, another risk (ibid), which might result in an individualized and inflated anticipation of individual agency.

My understanding of identity emerging paradoxically in processes of interdependency will inevitably lead to ambiguous expectations followed by contradictory and mixed emotions. Inability to find ways of *being with oneself in another* and therefore not living up to expectations from either self or others might lead to feelings of shame, embarrassment, disappointment and humiliation (Simpson & Marshall, 2010:352), while at the same time meeting other expectations might lead to a more positive emotional response. Such mixed embodied emotions are illustrated in all my narratives, where in my P2 I felt confident to engage with the conflict, while at the same time intimidated by the anxiety it provoked in the participants, in my P3, I was unhappy to feel invisible, however proud to be invited into many assignments. In my P4, I closely connected to the group and shortly after felt alienated and disappointed about the response I received from them.

My understanding of human interaction, however, does not only include interaction with other people. With Lefebvre´s perspective on space, I also argue how a wider understanding of the spatial elements influences identity processes. As illustrated in my P4, the interactions in the room with formal seating, microphones, and pictures of former mayors on the wall affected my ability to engage as a participant equally to the others. They affected my way of relating, and I claim that relationships with both other people and spatial settings play a role in negotiating identity. In this sense, identities are uncontrollable and emerge when human bodies interact in time and space.

**Argument 2: Paradoxically, there is a greater potential for freedom within the emergence of leadership with the acceptance and exploration of interdependencies. In doing so, we more fully recognize ourselves and others through resonant relationships.**

The above-argued paradox between the individual and the social involves accepting our interdependencies in which leaders are entangled. The idea is that we can never be liberated but only get a sense of degrees of freedom when engaging with the ongoing enabling and constraining we experience. This aims at the importance of continuing inquiry into present power relations and ongoing rhythms of everyday organizational life as an opportunity to explore the potential for freedom.

The paradoxical approach challenges how the mainstream understanding of leadership tends to be based on binary terms and dualisms. Paradox studies has been increasingly adopted by management scholars and is generally treated as an alternative way of inquiring into tensions and contradictions in organisational life, focusing on how we can attend to competing demands simultaneously, as argued by Smith & Lewis (2011:381).  The paradoxical approach to tensions is addressed in diverse ways e.g., by the use of different labels such as paradox, dialectics and dualities (Smith et. al., 2017:7). Bouchikhi argues that finding balance or organisational equilibrium between dialectical dimensions is central to managers' concerns and that they have the power to shape a context where contradictory forces can result in effectiveness and progress instead of anarchy and decline (1998:230). Others argue that leaders can reduce negative feelings and rebalance priorities by acting as sensegivers in relation to followers (Lüscher & Lewis, 2008, Sparr, 2018). A common quest is to understand when leaders fail to harmonize by emphasizing one pole rather than another instead of integrating inherent paradoxes (Clegg, Cuhna & Cunha, 2002, Peng & Nisbett, 1999).

Cunha and Putnam argue how scholars engaging with paradox generally agree that a *both-and* approach, in favor of thinking *either-or,* will foster creativity, enable virtuous circles and result in successful outcomes over time (2019:97). They also problematize the conceptual looseness in the use of paradox as an umbrella for exploring close yet distinct concepts that map all organizational tensions and contradictions.  Smith et. al. argue that management scholars have used the paradox framework to successfully unpack a variety of organizational phenomena, contributing to debates by arguing that paradox is not a contingency question but is the simultaneous presence of contradictions that are mutually codependent (2017:vi). They introduce a unifying approach to paradox, in which they agree on paradox as two interwoven and constitutive features that makes the tensions different and more complex than other tensions, such as dilemmas or competing demands, as examples (2017:vi).

In this thesis, I use a paradox framework to unpack freedom as an organisational phenomenon rather than theorizing about paradox myself, but it might be useful if I clarify how I stand in relation to this debate. I am taking a pragmatist perspective on paradox, where I distinguish between paradox, dialectics and chiasms as elaborated in my P3 (pp. 80-88). I relate dialectics and chiasms to two opposites that seem to coexist and draw on the understanding of paradox as two negating yet simultaneously mutually constituting ideas (as explained by Mowles, 2015:33), while looking at what it reveals about the theme of freedom. In this sense, I oppose the dichotomy in the understanding of both-and (agreeing with Griffin, 2002:10 and as I argued in my P2 and P4).

I oppose the idea that leaders can control the future and through this ensure balance or organisational equilibrium but argue that these ambiguities are an immanent and significant part of organisational life, deserving of our attention and understanding. From a pragmatist perspective, I also agree with Putnam & Cunha when they emphasize that scholars might treat responses of either/or, both/and as repertoires of dealing with multiple types of contradictions that emerges between members of organisations (2019: 97), and that these responses are important to continuingly inquire into.

I agree with the critique of how the distinctions, e.g., between leaders and followers, can be regarded as problematic and concerning (Collinson, 2005:1435).  I agree with the scholars who argue that thinking in dualisms prevents us from acknowledging the contradictory, ambiguous, multiple, and blurry character of the power relations in which leadership identities emerge and change (ibid). According to Alvesson & Kärremann, even theories that move away from thinking about leaders as heroes or villains assume that leadership is attributed to idealized faith in the positive outcomes, such as harmony, effectiveness, and moral order, leadership can provide (2016:142). Further arguments elaborate how the movement away from the understanding of the heroic leader still emphasizes the paradigm of the charismatic leader, who remains unaffected by the organization and can offer a way out of present problems (Spoelstra, 2019:3). In addition, Mowles argues how the dominant theories of managerial intervention within an organisation are based on system dynamics, assuming that organisations are self-regulating. Simultaneously, the manager is a detached, objective observer who can intervene to help the followers bring about the necessary change (2011:31).

My argument resonates with Collinson´s approach to the dialectics of leadership. He also highlights a paradoxical relation between managers and organisations and a need to explore how subjectivities are being negotiated to further understand the complexity of these processes (2005:1435). Even though I emphasize how relations are between human beings and that organisations are all about human bodies relating, the paradoxical perspective challenges the dichotomy between leaders and followers. I question the idea of the autonomous leader. However, I also oppose the understanding of leaders as being without agency and primarily formed by social structures. As a result, I argue that freedom within leadership comes with acknowledging the interdependencies as they are described in my first argument. My argument is that leaders *can* find degrees of freedom within the power relations in which they get entangled but never experience complete freedom.

Freedom in this sense is not the freedom *from* constraints however, the freedom *to* engage with the idea that we are both enabled and constrained in the negotiations of identity and our everyday leadership practice. This approach is closely connected with the understanding of power. In my P2, I draw on Foucault and Elias´ perspective on power to argue how power is not individually held. Both present an understanding of the constraining and disciplining character of our social lives while at the same time emphasizing the productive and enabling forces of power (Foucault, 1976, 1978, 1982 & Elias, 1970, 1991). In this way, I move away from the notion that power is a force held over others but take the perspective that power is closely connected with practice and enables agents or leaders to act and make a difference in the world by intervening (Allen, 2008:1614). The idea that we are simultaneously both enabled and constrained in our everyday leadership practice is a cornerstone in my perspective on freedom, which relies on human interdependencies.

As illustrated in my P2, my ability to stay with the conflict enabled the participants to talk about what was going on between them. However, at the same time, it seemed constraining since it left them helpless in order to find ways to continue the process afterwards. The power to make a difference can, in this way, as easily lead to domination and constraint as it does to enabling and the greater good (ibid). To experience freedom within leadership is, in this perspective, to draw attention to our social interactions and comes with the paradoxical sense of self and others. The split between leaders and followers and the ideas of the charismatic leader expressing a strong emphasis on leadership as good-doing (Alvesson & Kärremann, 2016:140) might in itself be constraining for our sense of freedom within our practice of leadership. In my P4, I felt positioned as the single person responsible for the process, which made me feel alienated from the other participants and unable to engage openly.

Recognizing the mutual dependencies comes, in my perspective, from a close relation to both self and others. Paying attention to the ongoing interactions relates to my perspective on resonant relationships, where we stay open to ourselves and the otherness of others. I draw on Rosa (2019) and Bernstein (1991) when emphasizing the necessity of close relationships to experience a sense of freedom. Rosa describes resonant relationships as experiences when we are both moved by the world and moving it at the same time by taking the Hegelian perspective on how subject and world interpenetrate while permeating both sides, which, according to Rosa, holds on to the mystery in terms of Hegel´s "world-spirit" (2019:316). In this way, resonance is not the removal of ambiguity but a way of exploring the contradictory character of our relationship with others.  Not suppressing the otherness of others, but willingly listening to whatever emerges in our ongoing interactions to seek mutual, reciprocal understanding (Bernstein, 1991:337) then becomes central in our efforts to freely engage with the enabling and constraining in which we are entangled.

When I experience indeterminacy in my P3, I draw on Hegel´s perspective on *being with oneself in another* (Honneth, 2000:27), which emphasizes not suppressing the sense of self. Taking this perspective, which I address as determinate indeterminacy, is a way of understanding resonant relationships with oneself and others. Additional to relating openly to others, I argue how leaders simultaneously more actively take themselves as an object to themselves. This point means that we inquire into the paradoxical relation between self and others and the mutual dependencies we are formed by and forming. One could think of this as a double paradox in the sense that we become selves because there are other selves, and at the same time, we can take ourselves as objects to ourselves reflexively. In this sense, the paradoxical relationship is both between self and others and involved in our ongoing reflexive relation to ourselves as both subject and object. Such a process is illustrated in the collaboration at the DMan community meetings and the learning set, as explained in the methodology section.

I here draw on Dewey´s perspective when he claims that freedom can be acquired when developing new ways of relating to one's own behaviour (Brinkmann, 2013:148). As an example, I was in an internal meeting at the University college discussing how our research could be more integrated into our teaching. When the research manager suggested that more researchers should be involved in planning the education, I felt a knot in my stomach. Instead of just resisting this suggestion, I shared the feeling this evoked in me and tried to elaborate on why I reacted in this way. I explained how I was worried about how researchers might not be familiar with the progression of the education and my fear about how this would make the education less cohesive. Bernstein draws on Arendt and presents the idea that freedom *"is the positive achievement of human action and exists only as so long as that public space exists in which individuals debate together and participate with each other in determining public affairs"* (Bernstein, 1983:209) becomes central in our ongoing efforts of gaining a sense of both self and others. The idea of leaders being detached might lead to a lack of understanding of the mutual dependencies, a sense of alienation with the results of feeling powerless or unfree. At this meeting in my practice, I found how sharing my concerns was not perceived by the others as resisting the idea, but they seemed to welcome my worries even though they challenged the suggestion from the manager.  In my P4, this is expressed when I feel disappointed by the conversations and unable to explore the suggestions to find fixed solutions, such as creating an informational system. Simultaneously, I did not share the emotional reactions this evoked in me.

In summary, I argue how the first step of participating in public discussions is to accept one's struggles and puzzles and share the contradictions and ambiguities we experience by holding on to our sense of self while simultaneously staying open to the otherness of others. In this way, I argue that one might find greater freedom paradoxically by recognizing and working with interdependencies through resonant relationships within which we listen and stay open, i.e. to differences. I do not suggest that one should constantly share struggles and emotions publicly. However, I argue that whether or when to share is based on a judgment about whether sharing might be helpful for self and others.

**Argument 3: Leaders need to pay attention to their engagement with recurrent idealisations, i.e. the contemporary pressure for speed in organizational life, which might contribute to the illusion of freedom through individual agency.**

My research indicates how leaders tend to get caught up in fixed idealisations about what leaders can or should be doing. One of the problems with this is that it creates unrealistic and impossible expectations constraining people into ways of engaging that, at best, distract or even alienate from reality. One example is the idea of enabling change, as illustrated in my P4, where the conversations were about problem-solving and not as reflexive as I had planned. I made sense of this situation as going in the wrong direction compared to the programme's ambitions. Instead of engaging with the patterns that emerged, I became frustrated. I got caught up in an idealisation of change in organisations and took repetitive communication patterns as constraining for change. Taking the dialectical perspective Lefevbre refers to in his rhythmanalysis, repetition both excludes differences and gives birth to them (2019:17). Subsequently to our experience from the meeting in my P4 narrative, we reflected on how the wish for change impacted our interaction with each other. In my ongoing work with the municipality, we continue to find ourselves slaves of the idealisation of change. However, this awareness and our ability to share our reflections about this experience help us move on together and improvise into this powerful pattern.

Working in the public sector in Denmark, I touch on the powerful impact of New Public Management and the thinking in terms of clients at my University College compared to earlier only thinking about students (e.g., in my P2). Several authors argue how this neoliberal paradigm has become an encompassing hegemonic project (Hoffmann, DeHart & Collier, 2006:10). Hartmann & Honneth claim that the neoliberal restructuring of the capitalist economic system exerts an individual pressure to adapt *"that does not undo the previously enumerated progressive processes, but durably transforms them in their function or significance"* (2006:49). Others point to the fact that the neoliberal perspective on subjects, markets, economic rationality, and competition brings a certain perspective on the concept of agency, where people own their skills and are to manage and develop these, which requires a managed reflexive stance in which people are objects to themselves (Gershon, 2011:539). However, Gershon argues that one is already alienated from oneself as an actor by facing oneself as a project that must be steered through various possible alliances and obstacles (ibid). This point resonates with Rosa´s idea of how our thinking of humans as resources might lead to alienation. Hartmann and Honneth further argue how *"the consequences for subjects can, on the one hand, be designated by the paradoxical concept of the compulsion to responsibility; on the other hand they can be grasped in psychological terms: the greater the responsibility individuals must assume for their life situations, the greater the danger the demands will be excessive"* (2006:52). The freedom that neoliberalism then offers seems to be a freedom to be an autonomous agent negotiating in a context where other agents are also ideally acting like business partners and competitors (Gershon, 2011:540). The understanding of autonomy is indeed considered a liberating idea by some. In contrast, my argument is that we can never escape from interdependency – the question is how these interdependencies are played out. My research shows how leaders sometimes fail to understand what impact they are likely to have when thinking about individuals and the organization instead of thinking about relationships and interdependencies.

As illustrated in P2, P3, and P4, I get caught up in focusing on outcomes and fashioning an intentioned future through my ways of interaction. My emphasis on the uncontrollability involved in organizational processes of the enabling and constraining in which leadership identities emerge criticizes the idea of splitting means and ends (Mowles, 2012). The conception of leadership within a neoliberal paradigm can be considered as the unique reflexive role of explaining to other autonomous entities how to manage themselves more successfully in a way where the self can correct and choose to remedy their unsuccessful self-management (Gershon, 2011:542). Several scholars point to the idea that public leadership, in what recent years has been called the competition-state in Denmark (Petersen, 2011, Kaspersen & Nørgaard, 2015), is undefined and how the position of leadership is up for constant negotiation (Petersen, 2008). The ambiguity and lack of clarity of what leadership concerns often come with the consequence of leaders running around a hamster wheel struggling to meet contradictive demands, often resulting in feeling inadequate and at risk of burnout (Kaspersen & Nørgaard, 2015). The expectations seem to be that the individual leader should navigate and find their own ways to adapt to this ambiguity through self-management. This point seems to idealize the individual freedom of the leaders while at the same time, deprive the leaders of taking responsibility for forming the conditions by which they find themselves constrained. My arguments oppose the idea of an authentic self who can simply choose to self-manage differently since it *"ignores the idea of multiple identities that are simultaneously salient and do not account for the evidence that dissonance and 'faking' can be tolerated and at times result in positive employee outcomes"* (O'Brien & Linehan, 2018:2). However, paying attention to how identities are being negotiated with others also entails understanding how globally patterns like neoliberalism constitute selves. As illustrated in my P4, where I turn reflexivity into a goal, the perception about making efforts to control outcomes comes with the risk of losing the paradox between self and others and the consequence of alienation. I got caught up in how I wanted the participants to self-manage.

Mowles argues how *"transformation is a process that constantly returns to self: Dewey wanted us continuously to keep ends and means, and the way that we habitually think about both, in view. In contemporary development discourse, in contrast, great claims are often made for the potential transformation of the lives of others"* (2012:552). In our struggles to experience freedom within leadership, I argue therefore, that we pay close attention to idealisations on leadership, such as controlling organizational outputs or the self-management of others and not thinking about either self or others as instruments or pure resources (Rosa, 2019:104). What I (and other leaders) can offer is an account of how I am thinking and struggling with present idealisations, contradictions, ambiguities, and dissonance. I get caught up and invite others to a collaborative in this exploration. In this way, leadership can be equated with doing research that collides with the need for speed as another idealisation in organizational processes.

Influenced by my reading of Lefebvre (1992) and Rosa (2010, 2019) and the perspective on rhythms and the acceleration of pace in life, I further argue how a contemporary perceived need for speed in organizational life can be perceived as a stumbling block in our struggles to experience freedom within our everyday leadership practice. Inquiring into present rhythms and inviting those present to resonant relationships in an attempt to avoid that *"subject and world confront each other with indifference or hostility and thus without any inner connection"* (2019:184), requires according to my research, a break with the need for speed.

In a study of the lives of organizational consultants, Stein argues *"that one of the principal products of their labour is to accelerate the working lives of others. Consultants often get hired by managers to speed up processes and staff. In order to do so, they need to establish modes of analysis and kinds of relations that constantly evaluate labour with reference to its temporal attributes"* (2018:104). In my P4, when I argue how freedom is to engage in close relations with both self and others, both enabling and constraining, and share participation and conversation, which might or might not result in resonance or liberation, my claim is that the process of gaining detachment to our involvement in power relations takes time. As illustrated in my P3, I was also caught up with speed regarding my performance with an overload of work and still refusing to reduce my number of assignments, with the result of indeterminacy and lack of thriving. This point relates to Brinkmann´s argument about how the pressure to self-improve has become an endless claim of contemporary human life, leading us to overbook our lives with projects to optimize our capacity (Brinkmann, 2014: 60). He argues how the idealisation of self-realisation relies on the idea of the autonomous individual, which in his perspective does not lead to liberation (2014: 31). In my argument, this allows us to identify how we are entangled in various powerful discourses and how freedom comes with the acceptance of how we can engage with the ongoing enabling and constraining that follows.

I argue for the need to pay attention to emerging idealisations and to challenge or break with some of them in order for both selves and others to experience the freedom to engage with the fact that we are continuously and simultaneously both enabled and constrained, which is not the same as being liberated from powerful patterns or even idealisations. However, to find degrees of freedom, we must relate reflexively to how we tend to get caught up in these power relations and how we can find ways of being collaboratively with ourselves in the communities to which we belong. This point is not a general opposition towards idealisations, but rather an attempt to pay attention to and try to break with those that seem unhelpful in our way of moving on together in our everyday work life.

Leaders cannot claim or enable resonance, but the idea of a leader's responsibility to invite people into a different relationship must be considered a specific philosophical stance in which we might experience resonance or alienation. Taking whatever experience we meet to explore and experiment with new ways of moving on together becomes a cornerstone in leadership practice.  In this way, leadership becomes an ethical obligation towards both self and others to pay attention to the interdependencies and find ways of engaging with both one's own interest and the interests of others in mind.

# Contributions of this thesis

My research makes a general contribution to understanding the struggles for freedom involved in identity processes within leadership in the public sector in Denmark. Based on my autoethnographically account of my own experience of conducting temporary leadership, I make plausible claims that I am confident can resonate with the experiences of public leaders in Denmark and of leaders in similar contexts such as the public sector in countries similar to Denmark.

The requirements for a professional doctorate in the DMan programme entail an explanation of the contributions of the thesis regarding knowledge and practice. This could indicate a dualism between theory and practice. However, throughout my thesis, I argue against dualisms and how such approaches are not conducive to a complex understanding. Writing this section, I find it important to underline how my whole thesis relies on a non-dichotomy between knowledge and action. When I now turn to elaborate on the contributions, I draw on Dewey´s perspective that the difference between theory and practice is a difference between two kinds of practice (Brinkmann, 2013:65). My argument is then that the movement in theorising and the movement in practice, which I describe in the following, should be perceived as mutually constituted.

## Contributions to knowledge

My research demonstrates the importance and relevance of taking a paradoxical perspective on understanding leadership identity and on people´s simultaneous wish to belong to communities while still maintaining a sense of freedom related to the need to stand out as individuals. My argument considers that the identity work involved with the development of leadership practice is about negotiations of our degrees of freedom. i assert how the paradoxical perspective to these processes and the acceptance of interdependency are important aspects of experiencing a degree of freedom in our relationship with others. Building on Elias and Mead, I oppose the dichotomic approach to leadership and followers and the separation of leaders from cultural structures in organizations but emphasize the mutual paradoxical relation between the self and the social. I point to a double paradox between the self and the self, taking oneself as an object to oneself and between self and other selves.

Understanding identity paradoxically is not novel. However, interweaving this perspective with an emphasis on the emergence of identities based on rhythmanalysis elaborates on this perspective. The contribution is the explanation of identities as both temporal and spatial (Lefebvre, 1992), emphasizing the blurry, ambiguous and contradictory character of belonging to different groups and the entanglement in different norms and rhythms, which unfolds the volatile character of identity that comes from being simultaneously formed by and forming the social. The thesis does not contribute to debates on defining paradox, however, my focus on understanding leaders' struggles for freedom from a paradoxical perspective does add to existing paradox research and constitute an argument in favour of the need for researchers to make visible the invisible currents of paradox (Smith, Lewis, Jarzabkowski & Langley, 2017:vii).

Further, I emphasize how the uncontrollability involved with the social process of leadership is played out in everyday organizational life, however still providing individuals opportunities to influence these processes. This point leads to the second contribution opposing the understanding of freedom within leadership as liberation from constraints. Drawing on Bernstein´s interpretation of Arendt (Bernstein, 1983), this thesis highlights the paradoxical relation between self and others which leads to the understanding of freedom, not *from* our interdependency with others, but as the freedom *to* engage with the acceptance that we are continuingly and simultaneously both enabled and constrained. Finding our ways of interacting and improvising into present rhythms and power relations is closely connected to the experience of freedom based on the Hegelian perspective on *being with oneself in another* (Honneth, 2000).

The struggle for freedom in everyday leadership is closely connected with holding on to the paradoxical perspective on self and others and staying in relation in order to be able to experience ourselves with others. A perception of freedom *from* indicates a break in our relation to others, while the understanding of freedom *to* holds on to the relation. Therefore, the third contribution of this thesis is an approach to understanding leadership as research, arguing how the inquiry into the ongoing interdependency with others inevitably must be part of everyday leadership practice. The reflexive exploration of the mutual dependencies in which we get caught up might lead to a sense of freedom to find ways of participating. To stay in relation with others and engage in a mutual reflexive inquiry becomes an important part of leadership practice and our ability to find agency in complex situations.

The fourth contribution of this thesis addresses how contemporary dominant understandings of leadership in the public sector in Denmark and the ideas of organizational life can be seen as stumbling blocks regarding the struggles to experience freedom. My research shows how the accelerating pace, the need for speed in achieving goals, and the focus on humans as resources come with the risk of alienation from both self and others, as suggested by Rosa. Engaging in resonant relationships requires time to inquire and a break with the idea that leaders can control outcomes. I assert that we get caught up in idealisations, and my research shows how some of them might reinforce the risk of alienation and indeterminacy and, through this, a lack of agency and a weak sense of freedom. The interweaving of these different aspects brings a novel nuance to the understanding of freedom in the identity work of leaders and offers a perspective on leadership as related to research.

With the influence from the perspective on complex responsive processes of human relating, my research further contributes to understanding these processes by considering the emergence of leadership as negotiations of degrees of freedom in everyday practice. The elaboration of the identity work of leaders focusing Lefebvre´s rhythm analysis and the focus on human bodies interacting with inspiration from Merleau-Ponty combined with the contemporary conditions on which basis degrees of freedom is negotiated adds yet another perspective to the interdisciplinary approach to the complex responsive processes of human relating in organizational life.

## Contributions to practice

During the last three years, the process of doing research has been closely connected with my practice. In this section, I reflect on the movement in my practice, as I have experienced it and from the experience of others. Sharing my movements in practice might be beneficial or inspiring to other people working within leadership processes.

My presentation of the multi-roled character of my job in the introduction to this thesis comes with the result of my thesis also pointing towards many audiences. My thesis is about leadership, but in the way I perceive this, the contributions to practice can also be related to the work of both teachers and consultants.

Acknowledging the ambiguity and contradictory character of organizational life has made me far less afraid of the different conflicts that might arise. I even find myself encouraging myself and others to explore these and through this depathologising of conflict. Based on my experience in my P2, I take a stand in believing that engaging with emerging conflicts might be helpful. I am aware that other people might experience anxiety-provoking and even violent situations when I chose to pay attention to conflictual situations.  These points have made me, at the same time, more insistent in my invitation into such reflections, however, at the same time, I am aware of the response I get from others to find ways of taking my own interest and the interest of others seriously. Another change is that I am increasingly bringing my own emotional reactions and the power struggles I myself experience into conversations with leaders. I still tend to get caught up in my habitual ways of thinking about how I should not pay too much attention to myself, but I find myself challenging this pattern and continue to be surprised when other people find my sharing helpful. When to share my own emotions and struggles or invite others to do so is based on an ongoing judgment about whether this might be helpful in the situation, as I am also aware of how this might make it less possible for people to move on together. These judgements can be difficult and I sometimes regret my choices when I experience unexpected response from others.

Gradually, I find that my pattern of wanting to belong to many groups is changing. In conversations with some of my colleagues at the University College, they indicate how I have become very clear in my understanding of what we are able, or maybe more precisely unable, to do with the leaders with whom we work. I recognize this in my stronger ability to say no to assignments, that require a certain predetermined output and more able to present alternative approaches to the work I do. In negotiations of new assignments, I find myself more confident to share that I will not be able to implement or control specific outcomes, but what I can do is participate in sharing my knowledge, experience and inviting them into exploratory conversations and interaction. In this way, I have become more critical of which communities I want to belong to as a freedom to choose my way of engaging with others.

Another colleague explained that she experienced me as much more critical in my general approach to our work, which resonates with my own experience of being less indeterminate. My pattern of indeterminacy seems to have changed as I have described in my P4 from the understanding of determinate indeterminacy. I still insist on staying open to others, but it has become easier for me to gain detachment from my involvement with others and as a result avoid thinking that disagreement or dissonance means a break in my relations with others. Taking a stand of my own, being critical towards others might or might not lead to exclusion. I find it easier to engage with the uncontrollability involved in these processes.

My stronger critical approach also makes me doubt my own practice, where I find it increasingly difficult to meet the current expectations of the work I carry. Working with leaders in the public sector in Denmark is still largely concerned with ideas of controlling outputs and speeding up processes of implementing change. When refusing to adapt to these paradigms, instead of challenging them, I find myself doubtful about how to continue this kind of work. However, in being more clear about my own stand, there seem to be possibilities to work with people who also feel the need to challenge these ideas and find alternative ways of working.  Subsequently, I see my struggle for freedom combined with an ongoing obligation to speak in the public domain about my own stance, even if it collides with powerful discourses, not because I think I can control the result, but in order to engage in the democratic conversation and with the confidence that we become who we are in close relationships with others.

Finally, I practice leadership based on ongoing research into the present micro interactions that emerge in my everyday work life. My ethical stance is to pay attention to those issues continuously. Autoethnography has in this way changed from being an approach to research methodology to my way to practice everyday leadership. I am member of a group of former students from the DMan, in which we continue to share narratives about our practices to make sense of our experiences. Furthermore, I often invite the managers I work with to share narratives from their practice, both in writing and orally. This has become a significant way of my working with the managers to explore how they can find degrees of freedom in their leadership practice.

With the arguments of this thesis, I emphasize the role of research in everyday leadership practice and the endeavor to continuously inquire into organisational rhythms of time and space. By acknowledging how leadership identities emerge paradoxically in relation to others, and by continuously inquiring into these interdependent processes, leaders might find degrees of freedom to interact. Relating reflexively to the complexity of the power relations leaders get caught up with creates an insight into how we are simultaneously both formed by and forming what is going on in everyday organizational life. By understanding our own practice as emerging from the paradox of individual and social experiences of, for example, ambiguity and contradictory feelings as leaders might not be placed solely in the individual but understood as a social practice shared with others. By sharing these experiences with others, leaders and facilitators of leadership development might contribute to more resonant relationships and avoid what Rosa refers to as relations of relationlessness (2019) and thereby gain a stronger sense of self, based on resonant relationships.

I have moved away from thinking of myself as a neutral facilitator of other peoples learning processes and identity work and towards an understanding of participation. By giving a clearer account of myself, how I come to think and feel in my interaction with the people I work with, I enable others to recognize themselves. I try to reject the invitation to present the truth about how to practice leadership, but I do present my own way of navigating the complexity in which we get involved and the difficulties I find in doing so. By sharing my struggles, I find that it becomes easier for others to share theirs and to some extend the idea that we share some difficulties seem to be helpful in not placing the problems in the individual. Even when we do not share the same experience, and allowing the dissonance to show, it seems to help us move on together.  An example from my ongoing work with the group of managers from the narrative in P4 was a meeting when I presented my perspective on what I find challenging in collaborating with others. One of the managers responded that she did not find it difficult at all and how we should stop problematizing. Instead of feeling criticized or thinking of her as resistant, I found myself curious and exploring her experience by asking her to say more about it. This turned into a conversation in the group where the other managers shared their stories about very different experiences in collaboration with others. Nobody seemed to have the exact same understanding, but by sharing, we became visible for each other, and we became more aware of the differences in the group with which we are to collaborate.

When taking on both formal and temporary leadership positions, I see now how I (and others) can become more visible to both ourselves and others through curiosity, exploration and reflexivity, when we accept ambiguities and different ways to navigate the contradictory character of organisational life. Instead of idealizing one way over another, I find how I and other leaders can more fully understand dissonance and through this find our own way of interacting with the fact that we are both enabled and constrained in different ways.  My experience of gaining understanding, and through this a stronger sense of self in these processes, seem to resonate with other leaders, consultants, and facilitators and can contribute to their practice as well. An example is how an understanding of different perceptions of the requirements of e.g., pace in leadership development processes enabled us to spend more time with conversation as illustrated in my P4. In this way my practice is not only an invitation to share how we experience e.g. collaboration, but also to share our doubts about whether or how to challenge hegemonic truths.

Collaborative exploration of interdependencies might also help leaders at an experiential level to navigate organisational paradoxes, ambiguities and contradictions and maybe even to challenge some of the idealisations about leadership and organisational life, which we find ourselves constrained by. Through such processes, leaders might experience degrees of freedom and agency in their interaction with others.

# Further research

As mentioned in my methodology, my research aims not to arrive at an exhaustive understanding of my theme, which has also made me deselect other adjacent topics of inquiry. As such, this thesis opens to further inquiry.

My research is problem-driven and based on my experiences with the people with whom I work. My experience of being a woman and how gendered aspects in negotiating leadership identity might or might not be played out in everyday organizational practice could be an interesting opportunity for further exploration.

I inquire into my practice within the public sector in Denmark and refer to the impact of the Danish *Law of Jante*. The extent to which leadership identities emerge differently in Denmark compared to other countries might also be interesting.

In my thesis, I briefly touch on the idea that the acceptance of a mutual interdependency between the individual and the social comes with an ethical obligation to the practice of leadership. The idea of leaders being formed by others and simultaneously forming the social addresses another aspect of whether leaders carry a specific ethical task and what this process might entail.

As the conditions of leadership keep changing, currently with Covid and the rise of populism as just two examples, inquiry into leadership will always be incomplete which implies the ongoing need for further research.

With the experience of researching this thesis, I am certain that several other ideas for further research will emerge in my ongoing practice. As such, I more than before consider myself a researcher – not as a task or a role, but more as a stance in how I relate to my own ongoing experiences.

# Bibliography


Allen, John; 2008, Pragmatism and power, or power to make a difference in a radically contingent world, ScienceDirect, Geoforum, 39, pp. 1613-1624

Alvesson, Mats & Svenningsson, Stefan; 2003, Good Visions, Bad Micro-management and Ugly Ambibuity: Contradictions of (Non-)Leadership in a Knowledge-Intensive Organization, Organization Studies, vol. 24(6), pp. 961-988

Alvesson, Mats, Bridgeman, Todd, & Willmott, Hugh; 2009, The Oxford Handbook on Critical Management Studies, Oxford University Press, Oxford

Alvesson, Mats, Loacker, Bernadette & Sandberg, Jörgen; 2013, Process here, there and everywhere: Entangle the multiple meanings of ´process´ in identity studies, Paper submitted to the Fifth International Symposium on Process Organization Studies, 20-22th of June, 2013, Crete

Alvesson, Mats & Kärreman, Dan; 2016, Intellectual Failure and Ideological Succes in Organization studies: The Case of Transformational Leadership, Journal of Management Inquiry, vol. 25(2) pp. 139-152

Alvesson, Mats & Sköldberg, Kaj; 2018, Reflexive Methodology – New Vistas for Qualitative Research, Sage, London

Andersen, Tom; 1994, The reflecting team – Dialogues and Dialogues about the Dialogues, W. W. Norton & Company, New York

Anderson, Harlene; 1997, Conversation, Language and Possibilities, Basic Books, New York

Anderson & Gehart; 2007, Collaborative Therapy – Relationships and Conversations that make a Difference, Routledge, London

Antonacopoulou, Elena P.; 2014, The experience of learning in space and time, Prometheus, vol. 32(1), pp. 83-91

Baldwin, John D.; 1988, Habit, Emotion and Self-Conscious Action, Sociological Perspectives, vol. 31(1), pp. 35-58

Bachrach, Peter & Baratz, Morton; 1970, Power and Poverty, Oxford University Press, New York

Berg-Sørensen, Grøn & Hansen; 2011, Organiseringen af den offentlige sektor (Organizing the public sector) Hans Reitzels Forlag, Copenhagen

Bernstein, Richard J.; 1983, Beyond Objectivism and Relativism – Science, Hermeneutics and Praxis, University of Pennsylvania Press, Philadelphia

Bernstein, Richard J.; 1991, The New Constellation; The Ethical Horizons of Modernty/Postmodernty, Polity, Cambridge

Bernstein, Richard J.; 2016, Pragmatic Encounters, Routledge, New York

Bouchikhi, Hamid; 1998, Living with and Building on Complexity: A Constructivist Perspective on Organizations, Organization Articles, vol. 5(2), pp. 217-232

Bourdieu, Pierre & Wacquant, Loiic, J. D.; An invitation to Reflexive Sociology, The University of Chicago Press, Chicago

Bourdieu, Pierre; 1991, Language and Symbolic Power, Polity Press, Oxford

Bourdieu, Pierre; 1995, Distinksjonen, Pax Forlag, Oslo

Brinkmann, Svend; 2012, Qualitative Inquiry in Everyday Life – Working with Everyday Life Material, Sage Publications, London

Brinkmann, Svend; 2013, John Dewey – Science for a Changing World, Transaction Publishers, New Jersey

Brinkmann, Svend; 2014, Doing Without Data, Qualitative Inquiry, vol. 20(6), pp. 720-725

Brinkmann, Svend & Tanggaard, Lene; 2015, Kvalitative metoder (Qualitative methods), Hans Reitzels Forlag, Copenhagen

Brown, Andrew D.; 2017, Identity Work and Organizational Identification, International Journal of Management Reviews, vol. 19, pp. 296-317

Brown, Andrew D.; 2019, Identities in Organization Studies, Organizations Studies, vol. 40(1), pp. 7-21

Burr, Vivian; 1995, An introduction to Social Constructionism, Routledge, London

Burrell, G. & Morgan, G.; 1979, Sociological Paradigms and Organizational Analysis. Part I, In search of a framework, Ashgate Publishing Limited, Hants

Carrol, B & Nicholson, H.; 2014, Resistance and struggle in leadership development. Human Resources, vol 67(11), pp. 1413-1436

Clegg, Steward R., Cunha, João Vieira da & Cunha, Miguel Pina e; 2002, Managing paradoxes: A relational view, Human Relations, vol. 55(5), pp. 483-503

Collinson, David; 2005, Dialectics of Leadership, Human Relations, vol. 58(11), pp. 1419-1442

Cook, Gary A.; 1993, George Herbert Mead – The making of a social pragmatist, University of Illinois Press, Urbana & Chicago

Cooperrider, David L. & Whitney, Diane 2005, Appreciative Inquiry – A positive Revolution in Change, Berrett-Koehler Publishers inc., San Francisco

Cunha, Miguel Pina e & Putnam, Linda L.; 2019, Paradox theory and the paradox of success, Strategic Organization, vol. 17(1), pp. 95-106

Cunliffe, Ann L. & Jun, Jong S.; 2005, The need for reflexivity in public administration, Administration & Society, vol. 37(2), pp. 225-242

Cyert, R. & March, J.; 1963, A behavioral theory of the firm, Prentice Hall, New Jersey

Czarniawska, B.; 2004, Narratives in Social Science Research, SAGE Publications Ltd, London

Dahl, Robert A.; The Concept of Power, Behavioral Science, vol 2, pp. 201-215

Danelund & Jørgensen; 2009, Kompetencebroen (Bridge of competences), del II og III, Forlaget Metropol, Copenhagen

Danelund, Jørgen; 2009, Ledelse med mening (Leadership with meaning) Forlaget Metropol, Copenhagen

Danelund & Sanderhage;2012, Medledelse med muligheder (Co-leadership with possibilities), Forlaget Metropol, Copenhagen

Dewey, John; 1891, Moral theory and practice, International Journal of Ethics, vol. 1, pp. 186-203

Dewey, John; 1922, Human Nature and Conduct – An Introduction to Social Psychology, Theophania Publishing, Calgary

Dweck, Carol; 2006, Mindset – The New Psychology Of Success – How we can learn to fulfil our potential, Random House Publishing Group, New York

Elias, Norbert; 1970, What is Sociology?, University College Dublin Press, Dublin

Elias, Norbert; 1991, The Society of Individuals, Blackwell, Oxford

Elias, N. & Scotson, J. L.; 1994 (1965), The Established and the Outsiders, Sage, London

Elkjær, Bente; 2005, Når læring går på arbejde – et pragmatisk blik på læring i arbejdslivet (When learning goes to work – a pragmatist view on learning in work life), Samfundslitteratur, Copenhagen

Ellis, Carolyn, Adams, Tony E. & Bochner, Arthur E.; 2011, Autoethnography: An Overview, Historical Social Research, vol. 36(4), pp. 273-290

Fairhurst, Gail, T.; 2001, Dualisms in Leadership Research, in Jablin & Putnam, The New Handbook of Organisational Communication, Sage Publications Inc., pp. 379-439

Fairhurst, G. & Grant, D.; 2010, The Social Construction of Leadership: A Sailing Guide. Management Communication Quarterly, vol. 24(2), pp. 171–210

Fleck, Ludwik; 1979, Genesis and Development of a Scientific Fact, The University of Chicago Press, Chicago

Flyvbjerg, Bent; 1991, Rationalitet og magt (Rationality and power), Akademisk Forlag, Copenhagen

Flyvbjerg, Bent; 2001, Making Social Science Matter – Why social science fails and how it can succeed again, Cambridge University Press, Cambridge

Foucault, Michel; 1978 (1991), Discipline and Punish – The Birth of the Prison, Penguin, London

Foucault, Michel; 1982, The subject and Power, Critical Inquiry, vol. 8(4), pp. 777-795

Foucault, Mitchel; 1982a, Truth, Power, Self, Interview, Oct. 25, 1982, Posted on Michel Foucault's page on Facebook on the 29. th of november, 2017 https://www.facebook.com/MichelFoucaultAuthor/

Foucault, Michel; 1991 (1978), Discipline and Punish, Penguin Books, London

Foucault, Michel; 1994 (1976), Viljen til viden – Sexualitetens historie I (Danish translation of La Volonté de savoir), Det Lille Forlag, Copenhagen

Foucault, Michel; 1994-1999, The history of Sexuality Vol 1-3, Penguin Books, London

Foucault, Michel; 2000, The Archaeology of knowledge, Routledge, London

Gergen, Kenneth; 1991, The Saturated self: Dilemmas of Identity in Contemporary Life, Basic Books, New York

Gergen, Kenneth & Gergen, Mary; 2004, Social construction – Entering The Dialogue, Taos Institute Publications, Ohio

Gergen, Kenneth J.; 2009, Relational being – Beyond Self and Community, Oxford University Press, New York

Gershon, Ilana; 2011, Neoliberal Agency, Current Anthropology, vol. 52(4) pp. 537-555

Griffin, Douglas; 2002, The Emergence of leadership – Linking Self-organization to Ethics, Routledge, London

Hartmann, Martin & Honneth, Axel; 2006, Paradoxes of Capitalism, Constellations, vol. 13(1), pp. 41-58

Hay, Amanda; 2014, I don´t know what I am doing!: Surfacing struggles of managerial identity work, Management Learning, vol. 45(5), pp. 509-545

Heede, Dag; 2004, Det tomme menneske (The empty person), Museum Tusculanums Forlag, Charlottenlund

Helin, Jenny et. al.; 2014, The Oxford handbook of Process Philosophy & Organization Studies, Oxford University Press, Oxford

Hertzberg, Frederick; 1959, The motivation to work, Wiley, New York

Hochschild, Arlie Russel; 1983, The Managed Heart – Commercialization of Human Feeling, University of California Press, Berkeley

Hoffmann, Lisa, DeHart, Monica & Collier, Stephen; 2006, Notes on the Anthropology of Neoliberalism, Anthropology News, vol. 47(6), pp. 9-10

Holman Jones, Stacy, Adams, Tony E. & Ellis Carolyn; 2013, Handbook of Autoethnography, Left Coast Press Inc., California

Honneth, Axel; 2000, Suffering from indeterminacy – An Attempt at a Reactualization of Hegel´s Philosophy of Right, Van Gorcum, Amsterdam

Honneth, Axel and Margalit, Avishai; 2001, Recognition. Proceedings of the Aristotelian Society, Supplementary Volumes, Vol. 75, pp. 111-139

Hood, C.; 1991, A Public Management for All Seasons? Public Administration, vol. 69 (1), pp. 3-19

Hubbert, Paul; 2012, Journal of Management Education, Vol. 37(6), pp. 803-827

James, William; 1907 (1982), Pragmatism, Hackett Publishing Company, Indianapolis

Kaspersen, Lars Bo & Nørgaard, Jan; 2015, Ledelseskrise i konkurrencestaten (Leadership crisis in the competition state), Hans Reitzels Forlag, Copenhagen

Kennedy, F., Carrol, B. & Francoeur, J.; 2013, Mindset Not Skillset: Evaluating in New Paradigms of Leadership Development. Advances in Developing Humans Resources, vol. 15(1), pp. 10-26

Kingma, Sytze F., Dale, Karen & Wasserman, Varda; 2018, Organizational Space and Beyond – The Significance of Henri Lefebvre for Organization Studies, Routledge, New York

Knights, David & Clarke, Caroline A.; 2014, It´s a bittersweet Symphony, this Life: Fragile Academic Selves and Insecure Identities at Work, Organization Studies, Vol. 35(3), pp. 335-357

Kotter, John; 1995, Leading Change: Why Transformational Efforts Fail, Harvard Business Review, Vol. 73(2), pp. 59-67

Küpers, W.M.; 2013, Embodied inter-practices of leadership – Phenomenological perspectives on relational and responsive leading and following. Leadership, vol. 9(3), 335–357

Ladkin, D.; 2008, Leading Beautifully: How Mastery, Congruence and Purpose Create the Aesthetic of Embodied Leadership Practice. The Leadership Quarterly, vol 19, pp. 31-41

Lapadat, Judith C.; 2017, Ethics in Autoethnography and Collaborative Autoethnography, Qualitative Inquiry, vol. 23(8), pp. 589-603

Lave & Wenger; 1991, Situated learning: Legitimate peripheral participation, Cambridge University Press, Cambridge

Lefebvre, Henri; 2019, Rhythmanalysis – Space, Time and Everyday Life, Bloomsbury, London & New York

Low, Douglas; 2000, Merleau- Ponty's Last Vision – A proposal for the Completion of *The Visible and the Invisible*, Northwestern University Press, Evanston Illinois

Lukes, Steven; 1974, Power - A Radical View, Palgrave MacMillan, New York

Lüscher, Lotte S. & Lewis, Marianne W.; 2008, Organizational Change and Managerial Sensemaking: Working Through Paradox, Academy of Management Journal, vol. 51(2), PP. 221-204

Maslow, Abraham. H. (1954). *Motivation and Personality*, Harper and Row, New York

March, J, & Simon, H. A.; 1958, Organizations, Wiley, New York

Mead, George Herbert; 1925, The Genesis of the Self and Social Control, in A. J. Reck, Selected Writings: George Herbert Mead pp. 345-354

Mead, George Herbert; 1934, Mind Self and Society, Chicago University Press, Chicago

Mead, George Herbert; 1936, Movements of Thought in the Nineteenth Century, Chicago University Press, Chicago

Merleau-Ponty, Maurice; 1968, The Visible and the Invisible, Northwestern University studies in Phenomenology & Existential Philosophy, Evanston

Merleau-Ponty, Maurice; 2014(1945), Phenomenology of Perception, Routledge, London

Mowles, Chris; 2009, Consultancy as temporary leadership: negotiating power in everyday practice, Int. J. Learning and Change, vol. 3(3), pp. 281-293

Mowles, Chris; 2011, Rethinking Management – Radical Insights from the Complexity Sciences, Routledge, London and New York

Mowles, Chris; 2012, Keeping means and ends in view – Linking practical judgement, ethics and mergence, Journal of International Development, Vol. 24, pp. 544-555

Mowles, Chris; 2015, Managing in Uncertainty – Complexity and The Paradoxes of Everyday Organizational Life, Routledge, London and New York

Mowles, Chris; 2015a, Against Common Sense: managing amid the paradoxes of everyday life, text of a talk given by Chris Mowles at the University of Hertfordshire on Friday Feb 13th posted on the blog, Complexity and Management.com, in February 17, 2015

Muller, Robin M.; 2017, The Logic of the Chiasm in Merleau-Ponty´s Early Philosophy, Ergo – An open access, Journal of Philosophy, vol.4(7), pp. 181-227

Nordhaug, Odd; 1993, Kompetanse styring (Governing competence), Tano, Oslo

O´Brien, Elaine & Linehan, Carol; 2018, Problematizing the authentic self in conceptualizations of emotional dissonance, Human Relations, The Tavistock Institute, pp. 1-27

Pardales, M. J. & Girod, M.; 2006, Community of Inquiry: Its past and present future, Educational Philosophy and Theory, 38, vol.3, pp. 299-309

Petersen, Dorthe; 2008, Når ledelsespositionen er til forhandling – det dynamiske ledelsesrum: Myten of den suveræne leder (When the leadership position is up for negotiation – the dynamically room for leadership: The myth of the sovereign leader) in Erik Elgaard Sørensen; Ledelse og læring I organisationer (Leadership and learning in organisations) pp. 198-224, Hans Reitzels Forlag, Copenhagen

Pedersen, Dorthe, Greve, Carsten & Højlund, Holger; 2008, Genopfindelsen af den offentlige sektor – Ledelsesudfordringer i Reformernes tegn (The reinvention of the public sector – Leadership challenges in signs of the reforms), L&R Business, Copenhagen

Petersen, Ove K.; 2011, Konkurrence Staten (The Competition State), Hans Reitzels Forlag, Copenhagen

Piaget, Jean; 1952(1936), The Origin of Intelligence in the Child, Routledge & Kegan Paul, London

Piaget, Jean; 1973, Intelligensens psykologi (The psychology of intelligence) Hans Reitzels Forlag, Copenhagen

Putnam, Phillips and Chapman; 1999, Metaphors of Communication and Organization, in Managing Organizations, edited by Clegg, Hardy & Nord, SAGE Publishing, Thousand Oaks

Rennison, Betina Wolfgang; 2004, Ledelsesbegrebets historie I den offentlige sektor (The history of the concept of leadership in the public sector) in Offentlig Ledelse I Managementstaten (Public Leadership in the State of Management), edited by Dorte Pedersen, Samfundslitteratur, Copenhagen

Rogers, Carl; 1961, On Becoming a Person – a therapist´s view on psychotherapy, Houghton Mifflin Harcourt, Boston

Rorty, Richard; 1994, Towards a Liberal Utopia, Times Literary Supplement, 24, June, pp. 14

Rorty, Richard; 1999, Philosophy of Social Hope, Penguin, London

Rosa, Hartmut; 2010, Alienation and Acceleration – Towards a critical theory of late-modern temporality, NSU Press, Copenhagen

Rosa, Hartmut & Endres, Wolfgang; 2017, Resonanspædagogik – Når det knitrer i klasseværelset – Danish translation of Rezonanspådogogik - Wenn es im Klassenzimmer knistert. (Resonance pedagogy – when it crackles in the classroom), Hans Reitzels Forlag, Copenhagen

Rosa, Hartmut; 2019, Resonance – A Sociology of Our Relationship to the world, Polity Press, Cambridge

Sandemose, Aksel; 1933, En Flyktning Krysser sit Spor (A fugitive crosses his tracks), Norsk Forlag, Oslo

Schein, Edgar; 1985, Organizational Culture and Leadership, Jossey-Bass, San Francisco

Schein, Edgar; 1993, On dialogue, culture and organizational learning, Organizational Dynamics, vol. 22(2), pp. 40-51

Schön, D. A.; 1983, The reflective practitioner: How professionals think in action, Basic Books, New York

Shotter, John; 2015 Bevægelige verdener (moving realities), Forlaget Mindspace, Copenhagen

Simon & Chard; 2014, Systemic Inquiry – Innovations in Reflexive Practice Research, Everything is Connected Press, Farnhill

Simpson, Barbara & Marshall, Nick; 2010, The Mutuality of Emotion and Learning in Organizations, Journal of Management Inquiry, Vol. 19(4), pp. 351-365

Slife, B. D. & Richardson, F. C.; 2011, The relativism of Social Constructionism. Journal of Constructivist Psychology, vol. 24(4), pp. 333-339

Smith, Wendy K. & Lewis, Marianne W.; 2011, Toward a Theory of Paradox: A dynamic Equilibrium Model of Organizing, The Academi of Management Review, vol. 36(2), pp. 381-403

Smith, Wendy K., Lewis, Marianne W., Jarzabkowski, Paula & Langley, Ann; 2017, The Oxford Handbook of Organizational Paradox, Oxford University Press, Oxford

Sparr, Jennifer L.; Paradoxes in Organizational Change: The Crucial Role of Leaders´ Sensegiving, Journal of Change Management, vol. 18(2, pp. 162-180

Spoelstra, Sverre; 2019, The paradigm of the charismatic leader, Leadership, vol. 0(0), pp. 1-6

Stacey, Ralph, D.; 2003, Complexity and Group Processes – A Radically Social Understanding of Individuals, Routledge, London and New York

Stacey, Ralph & Griffin, Douglas; 2005, A Complexity Perspective on researching Organizations. Taking Experience seriously, Routledge, London

Stacey, Ralph; 2011, Strategic management and Organizational Dynamics – The challenge of Complexity, 6th edition, Prentice Hall

Stacey, Ralph and Mowles, Chris; 2016, Strategic Management and Organizational Dynamics – The challenge of complexity to ways of thinking about organisations, Pearson Education Limited, Harlow

Stein, Felix; 2018, Selling Speed: Management Consultants, Accelaration, and Temporal Angst, PoLAR – Political and Legal Anthropology Review, vol. 41(1), pp. 103-117

Stetsenko, Anna & Arievitch, M. Igor; 2004, The Self in Cultural-Historical Activity Theory – Reclaiming the Unity of Social and Individual Dimensions of Human Development, Theory & Psychology, vol. 14(4), pp. 475-503

Steyart, Chris; 1998, Human, All Too Human Resource Management - Constructing "the Subject" in HRM, unpublished manuscript, Papers in Organization No. 28, Copenhagen Business School

Taylor, Frederick W.;1914, The principles of Scientific Management, Harper & Brothers Publishers

Thomas, Gary; 2010, Doing Case Study: Abduction Not Induction, Phronesis Not Theory, Qualitative Inquiry, vol. 16(7), pp. 575-582

Thyssen, Ole; 1997, Værdiledelse – om organisationer og etik (Valuebased leadership –organisations and ethics), Gyldendal, Copenhagen

Thyssen, Ole; 1999, Kommunikation, kultur og etik (Communication, culture and ethics), DJØF Forlag, Copenhagen

Thøgersen, Ulla; 2015, Kropslighed og responsivitet: Shotter and Merleau Pontys fænomenologi (Embodyment and responsivity: The phenomenology of Shotter and Merleau Ponty) in John Shotter;  Bevægelige verdener, (Moving worlds) pp. 218—237, Forlaget Mindspace, Copenhagen

Vince, Russ; 2019, Institutional Illogics: The Unconscious and Institutional Analysis, Organization Studies, vol. 40(7), pp. 953-973

Vygotsky, L. S.; 1993, Studies on the history of behavior; Hillsdale, New Jersey

Weber, Max; 1968, Economy and Society - An outline of Interpretive Sociology, Bedminster Press, New York

Wenger, Etienne; 1998, Communities of Practice – Learning, Meaning and Identity, Cambridge University Press, Cambridge

Winkler, Ingo; 2018, Identity Work and Emotions: A Review, International Journal of Management Reviews, vol. 20, pp. 120-133

Åkerstrøm, Niels; 2001, Kærlighed og omstilling (Love and conversion), Nyt fra Samfundsvidenskaberne, Copenhagen

Åkerstrøm Andersen, Niels & Grønbæk Pors, Justine; 2014, Velfærdsledelse – Mellem styring og potentialisering (Leading welfare – Between management and potentialising), Hans Reitzels Forlag, Copenhagen